Kilcho

Farm Distillery or Family Dynasty?

By

Graham Ward

MAPLE
PUBLISHERS

Kilchoman - Farm Distillery or Family Dynasty?

Author: Graham Ward

First Published in 2025

ISBN 978-1-83538-591-3 (Paperback)
        978-1-83538-592-0 (E-Book)

Cover photos by Konrad Borkowski and Kilchoman, used with permission.

Book Cover Design and Layout by:
        White Magic Studios
        www.whitemagicstudios.co.uk

Published by:
        Maple Publishers
        Fairbourne Drive, Atterbury,
        Milton Keynes,
        MK10 9RG, UK
        www.maplepublishers.com

This book is written with the assistance of the Wills family and with contributions from employees, contractors and selling partners. Every effort has been made to faithfully reproduce the supplied information within this book and the Wills family were given the opportunity to read through the proof to correct any factual errors prior to publishing.

This book is dedicated to my great mate Tigga,
with whom I shared most of my whisky journeys,
including many to Islay.

CONTENTS

Chapter 1

Islay's history and the start of distilling

M uch has been written about whisky distilling on Islay, by people with much greater knowledge and ability to express themselves than me, but it is useful when considering the development and subsequent growth of Kilchoman, to look at why Islay malt whisky is so highly regarded, and why Kilchoman was the perfect place to introduce a new distillery at the time, way back in 2005.

Islay's history as far as it is known stretches back to around 8000 BC and possibly earlier. Its first inhabitants were from the Middle Stone Age – tools and implements discovered during investigations over the last 50 years have shown this. Some exhibits from the Mesolithic and Neolithic periods can be seen at the Museum of Islay Life in Port Charlotte. Archaeologists from Reading University, who now work in partnership with primary schools on Islay, found evidence of stone tools left by hunter gatherers, who would most likely have crossed the land bridge from Europe, as it was then, nearly 12,000 years ago.

There are many sites which evidence human existence on Islay throughout the pre-historic age. Dun Nosebridge is an Iron Age hill fort set on a rocky outcrop overlooking farmland east of Bridgend. There are around 80 similar Duns on Islay, but Dun Nosebridge is one of the largest and best-preserved. Burial chambers, like the Cragabus chambered cairn and standing stones scattered around the island, were used as markers and memorials.

The first major settlers on Islay were almost certainly Celts, drawn from different parts of Europe. Settlements were irregularly spread across Islay as there were large parts of the island where the land was not fertile enough to grow crops.

Islay formed part of the Gaelic kingdom of Dál Riata from the sixth century AD until around 300 years later, and Kildalton Cross was erected around 800 ADS, during this period. The cross still stands in the south-east of the island, beyond the Ardbeg distillery. The Vikings were the next occupiers, with the island remaining under Norse rule, creating independence for the Western Isles from the mainland.

It was around mid-12th century, when a rebellion under Somerled took place, against the Viking settlers, which brought the island back under Scotland's rule. When Somerled died in 1165, his lands were split between his three sons Donald, Rauri and Dougal. These men, and their followers each became responsible for the formation of three of Scotland's greatest clans - MacDonald, MacRuari, and MacDougall and they ruled Islay independently as 'Lords of the Isles', for several hundred years. They based themselves at Loch Finlaggan on the road to Port Askaig and ruins from the settlement are still visible today and well worth a visit (the site is now administered by the Finlaggan Trust).

During the Wars of Scottish Independence, the MacDonald and MacRuari clans backed Robert Bruce, while the MacDougall clan backed John Balliol. In 1493, John of Islay, Earl of Ross was forced to surrender his territories to King James IV of Scotland as recompense for his raid on Ross, and Islay came under direct Scottish rule.

During the 16th and 17th centuries clan rebellions across Scotland were commonplace. Historically, the largest and most important of the Highland clans was the Campbell clan, who were based in Argyll, which included ownership of Islay. Despite occupying a dominant position of power on mainland Scotland, Islay was presumably considered too far away, lacking in fertile land for crops and of little military importance, so it was mostly neglected by the Campbells, who acted largely as absentee lairds. As a result, the island failed to prosper for most of this period.

By the early 18th century, the Campbells struggled to maintain control over their estates on Islay due to low earnings and famine. A change of island ownership followed when a wealthy businessman and politician, Daniel Campbell of Shawfield, became laird. This was to be a welcome change for Islay as the economy began to thrive thanks to the improvement of farming methods and introduction of a textile industry.

The next generation continued to modernise the island with the construction of the village of Bowmore, the development of roads, a fishing industry, the provision of schools and the promotion of the church.

There are many theories as to when distilling started on Islay. Monks travelling over from Ireland are thought by many historians to have begun distillation on Islay, probably during the early fourteenth century, although estimations of the dates vary considerably. I prefer the MacBeatha hypothesis. The MacBeatha family travelled over from what is now Northern Ireland at some time around 1300 and settled in the Kilchoman parish.

They were physicians, who amongst other things, translated texts about distillation from Latin into Gaelic. The extension of this, although it has never been proven, was that Islay was the first place in Scotland to distil spirit and it was in the Kilchoman parish that it first occurred.

The island had limitless supplies of peat, and soft water in lochs and rivers made it an ideal location for distilling. On the fertile parts of the island, crofters grew bere barley (which is a low yielding barley able to be grown in soils with a low pH and grows quickly, helpful with the shortened summer experienced on Islay), which was for their own use, although any surplus was used for distillation.

Distilling was originally carried out openly until a tax was levied on whisky in 1644 as part of the Excise Act. This amounted to two shillings and eight pence per 'Scot's pint' (oddly this was almost half a gallon) of 'aquavitae' or other strong liquor. This forced the distillers to move into the remote glens and caves to avoid detection. The Mull of Oa peninsula was well known for illicit distilling, with stills found at Cragabus, Stremnishmore, Lower Killeyan and Goil. There were also stills at Octomore, Bridgend, Dail, Lossit, Tallant, Mulindry and many other isolated locations further North.

Even though the Excise Act was passed in 1644, none of the Crown's excisemen were permanently stationed on Islay until 1797, which allowed small scale distilling to continue for many years after other illegal distillers on the mainland were caught, and fined or imprisoned for similar practices. The 'Gaugers', as the excisemen were called, were reluctant to travel to Islay due to the 'wild and barbarous people' living there. Thankfully in the present day, the wildest thing that an Ileach (a native of Islay) is likely to do is to raise his hand in greeting as you drive past.

In 1777, the Reverend John McLeish of the Kilchoman Parish was reported as saying, ***"We have not an excise officer on the whole island. The quantity, therefore, of Islay whisky made here is very great and the evil that follows drinking to excess of this liquor, is very visible on the island."*** Sentiments not echoed by many islanders at the time, who considered the imposition of a tax to be an attack on their way of life, where, in such a harsh living environment, solace in alcohol was one of life's few pleasures.

What we know for sure is that Islay's first official whisky distillery was established at Bowmore in 1779.

The distilling of whisky on Islay during the late 18th and early 19th centuries, was responsible for a great deal of criminal activity. British historian Alfred Barnard wrote that a century earlier (his book The Whisky Distilleries of the United Kingdom was originally published in 1887, so reference is to late 18th/ early 19th Century) *'smuggling was the chief employment of the crofters and fishermen, more especially during the winter and many were the encounters that took place between them and the Government officers. Up to the year 1821 smuggling was a lucrative trade on Islay and large families were supported by it'.*

Islay whisky was smuggled to Argyllshire, Galloway (via the Mull of Kintyre and Ayrshire) and Ireland. It was also carried in small boats up the Forth of Clyde into Glasgow.

Excisemen patrolled the seas around Islay, sending armed raiding parties to find and destroy stills hidden in crofts, bothies and caves. Although the issue was endemic across the Island, the excisemen concentrated their efforts around the easier to reach Oa peninsula and along the south-east coast, around the areas we know now as the Ardbeg, Lagavulin and Laphroaig distilleries. It was rare for the customs officers to venture beyond Bowmore.

In the early 1800s, as there were now excisemen stationed on Islay, hundreds of individuals were accused of distilling privately, forcing many of Islay's illegal operators to register as distillers to avoid being fined and/ or imprisoned. Across the whole of Scotland at the start of the 1800's the authorities were confiscating more than 10,000 stills a year, yet the majority of whisky drunk still had no duty paid. The problem was widespread across the whole country and radical solutions were needed.

Following the conclusion of the Napoleonic Wars in 1815, the Crown's attention, especially due to its depleted coffers, once more returned to illegal distilling and there were renewed efforts to stamp out the illicit trade. Efforts were made to persuade some of Islay's more honest tenants to take out licences to distil. The issue for these small distilling operations, was not so much that they did not know how to distil whisky, (although the results were undoubtedly mixed around these times), but they lacked marketing and business skills and did not have the contacts to be able to sell their wares in a much wider market.

The 1823 Excise Act is widely recognised as enabling the establishment of the scotch whisky industry as we know it today. The Act reduced the previously punitive duties to two shillings and three pence per gallon (more than halving the previous duty) and distillers had to hold a licence costing 10 pounds. This opened access to not only the markets in Glasgow and Edinburgh, but more importantly to the market in England, which meant that distilling could take place on a much more significant scale and with bigger distilleries inevitably came economies of scale. Every distillery had to provide accommodation for a resident excise officer, as part of their obligations under the Act.

By 1836 fourteen Islay distillers were known to have moved from illegal distilling to paying their dues as a licensed distillery. Many of these smaller distilleries merged. Lagavulin was one such distillery, consisting originally of at least 10 small illicit distilleries and probably dating back to 1742, but official records list it as starting up in 1815.

Lots of small distilleries failed over a relatively short period of time or were acquired by whisky brokers and blenders from Glasgow and Edinburgh, who had seen the opportunities that larger scale production represented, especially with their contacts.

Port Ellen was acquired by John Ramsey, Chairman of the Glasgow Chamber of Commerce in 1820, Lagavulin by Glasgow Spirit Merchant, Alexander Graham in 1836, and Bowmore by the Glasgow blenders, William and James Mutter in 1837. Ardbeg was rescued from liquidation by Glasgow spirit merchant Thomas Buchanan, who purchased the distillery for £1,800 in 1838. Turbulent times indeed at the very start of more structured distilling on Islay. Interestingly the Port Charlotte Distillery was established in 1829, amongst all this turmoil.

The population on Islay peaked at about 15,000 sometime around 1841. Most of the population was engaged in subsistence farming, which was becoming more and more difficult. The Irish potato famine lasted seven years from 1845 and was symptomatic of the problems facing subsistence farmers around this time, many of whom were starving. Emigration became a major issue for the island in the latter half of the 19th century. Of those who remained, many went to the growing towns of Port Ellen and Bowmore and other larger villages, and the distilleries became a much more integral part of life on Islay.

The distillers, with their connections in Glasgow and Edinburgh, were able to lobby for better quality piers for the loading and offloading of wares and improved sea connections with the mainland. What had once been a collection of a few ramshackle dwellings grew into small coastal villages close to the distilleries. Ardbeg, being the farthest of the three southerly distilleries from Port Ellen at about 3.5 miles away, housed around 200 people and had its own post office, school and village hall. A new distillery at Caol Ila was initially established in 1846.

There is no doubt that in the 19th century, distilleries provided an income for hundreds of islanders and their families, but the jobs were mainly labouring and lower paid positions. Distilleries were generally run from the mainland, so there were few management roles available. Profits, after taxation, were usually returned to the owners on the mainland and were of no benefit to the community.

Blended whisky as we know it today was pioneered by Andrew Usher in Edinburgh, in the 1860's. By mixing single malt whiskies, which, compared to modern variants were raw and strongly flavoured, with grain whiskies (Aeneas Coffey patented his invention of the column still in 1830), blenders produced a whisky that was generally lighter and sweeter in character than the malt whiskies of the time. Islay whisky became much more popular in the 1870s and 1880s, as it provided rich, bold, peaty flavours for blended Scotch whiskies. New investors came to the island leading to the opening of Bruichladdich and Bunnahabhain in 1881, and the extension of existing facilities at the others.

Whisky in general and Islay whisky specifically has suffered periods of decline, which often went hand in hand with world events. After the Great War was the Great Depression of the late 1920s and '30s, with prohibition in the USA running from 1920 to 1933, and this meant long periods of closure for all distilleries. (Strangely the fortunes of Laphroaig improved during this period as they were able to export their whisky to the USA as a 'medicinal spirit'!). Port Charlotte closed its doors in 1929 and Port Ellen, mothballed that year, did not reopen until 1967 (and then closing some years later in 1983).

The Second World War also saw the closure of all distilleries due to a shortage of barley and manpower. There have been many other periods of hardship at the distilleries running through to the 1960's which saw men laid off and temporary closures.

The later 1960s and early '70s saw a rising interest in blended whisky and this led to a period of improved investment in distilleries on Islay. This only led to overproduction, which coupled with the high oil prices in the late 1970's, heralded a global economic decline and the associated reduction of disposable income created the 'whisky loch' of the early 1980s. Twenty distilleries closed their doors, many of them for good. Islay was by no means immune to this downturn, where Ardbeg was effectively closed from 1981 to 1996 (albeit producing some spirit during this time), Bunnahabhain from 1981 to 1984, Port Ellen closed and was demolished in 1983 and Bruichladdich closed sometime later in 1994, not re-opening until 2001.

It was around the time that Mark Reynier and his fellow directors re-established Bruichladdich in 2001 that a former wine buyer and independent whisky bottler first came up with the idea of setting up a new distillery on Islay, the first for 124 years. Anthony Wills had spent over thirty years in the drinks industry so had knowledge of how and where to sell his whisky but had little knowledge (a dangerous thing in itself) as to how to distil whisky. Over the course of the following chapters, I will discuss how this dream became a reality, the struggles along the way, the triumphs and failures, but most importantly, many of the people who established and maintain the Kilchoman brand.

⸺⊰⟨⟩⊱⸺

Chapter 2

Anthony and Kathy Wills

The Kilchoman story is on the surface about the desire of one man to create a distillery. Scratch the surface and you find it is a great deal more complex than that. Many other people have played a significant part in making this dream a reality, but none more so than the Wills family, whose own history is no less remarkable.

Anthony, was born in December 1956, and met Kathy through their mutual interest in sailing, when he was based in Bristol. Kathy's parents were located on the Isle of Wight, which provided him with the ideal opportunity to race every weekend. Whilst Anthony is modest about his sailing abilities, he took part in the third Whitbread Round the World yacht race in 1981/82 organised by the Royal Naval Sailing Association over 26,000 miles, as part of the crew of the FCF Challenger (an 80ft yacht), skippered by Les Williams.

To put in perspective the enormity of this challenge, 29 yachts started the race out of Southampton on 29 August 1981. They sailed from Southampton to Cape Town, from there to Auckland, then on to Mar Del Plata in Argentina, before completing the fourth leg to Portsmouth. An epic journey navigating some of the most dangerous waters on earth. Only 20 yachts finished the race out of the 29 that started it. The FCF Challenger finished 16th completing the challenge in over 138 days.

It says something about Anthony's strength of character, that he was able to take part in such a physical and mental challenge over four months and probably explains why he refused to be defeated by any of the challenges thrown up during the building and running of a distillery.

Anthony and Kathy were married in October 1983 and have three sons, George, James and Peter, all of whom are now heavily involved in the business. They also have four grandchildren, who may or may not continue with the family legacy. Time will tell no doubt.

Kathy's grandfather Spencer Wilks, served variously in positions including Managing Director, Chairman, and President of the Rover

Company from 1929 until the 1960s, having previously worked for Hillman Motor Company. He was involved in the design and building of the first Land Rover, with his brother Maurice, who at the time worked at Rover as Chief Engineer and Designer. Maurice had apparently been driving around his own farm on Anglesey in an old American-made Willys-Overland Jeep, and the two men used this as the inspiration to develop and produce a utility four-wheel-drive, as a vehicle for farmers/estates' management.

Legend has it that in 1947, while driving his heavily modified Rover 12 across the rugged Islay landscape, the estate's gamekeeper Ian Fraser remarked to Spencer that it must be a 'Land Rover'; thus, the name and a legend was born.

Even now that Land Rover is owned by Tata, the company embraces the story, and they come to Islay regularly to do promotional work. Kilchoman has maintained an involvement because of the family connection. This is shown not least in the Land Rover Tours that commenced in 2015, following a visit by Land Rover to the Distillery in 2014, as part of a sentimental return to the island where the model was first tested 67 years earlier.

Anthony's background is in the drinks industry, from the age of 22 until the current day. Initially he worked in the wine industry, for a range of companies, predominantly Allied Domecq and their various subsidiary companies in London. He worked for 12 years in London for wholesale wine businesses selling to supermarkets, restaurants, retailers and city businesses. In the late 70's and 80's, as we came out of recession in the UK, with more disposable income and eating out, it was a good time to be in wine sales.

By the late 1980's/early 1990's he was working for a co-operative French wine company as Sales Director, representing growers and chateaux from all over France selling out of France into the UK. At this time, Anthony could see that the market was developing rapidly towards major retailers (Majestic Wines for example was established in 1980) and supermarkets, and between them they gradually replaced all the smaller retailers, through pricing and competition.

By the early 1990's, Anthony became disenchanted at these developments as the enjoyment involved in the selling of fine wines was much diminished. Whilst he was working for a dynamic company, everything was being funnelled through the supermarkets and margins were tight. It was no longer providing him with any job satisfaction. As a family they were living in Bristol, the three boys were born between 1985 and 1989, and he was commuting to London, getting up at 6:00am and returning home at 9:00pm five days a week. Not a recipe for a happy family life.

He recalls that he was looking for a different life really, with a slower pace and shorter hours – Oh, the irony of that, looking back! Kathy's mother and father retired to Islay, having spent all their lives in the South of England, on the Isle of Wight. Kathy's family had always owned property on Islay on the Laggan Estate, which her grandparents had bought in the 1930s. She had been holidaying there with her family since she was a child. The Laggan estate was also used for the testing of the Land Rovers over many years. Despite having to sell the estate to pay death duties, the family retained the farmhouse.

Kathy unfortunately lost her mother quite suddenly in 1993. Anthony and Kathy had been considering moving anyway, so the decision to relocate the family to Scotland was made appreciably easier; despite having three very young boys they made the move in 1995. George, the eldest, would have been around ten at this time. They did not move to Islay, but to Colintraive, which is on the Cowal peninsula in the south of Argyll and Bute.

Following the move to Colintraive, Anthony made his first foray into the whisky industry. By the early 1990's independent bottlers were starting to get some recognition in the industry for their single casks. Most of the independents were doing single cask bottlings, but there was nothing particularly exciting. The premiumisation started in the 1990's and Anthony formed his own bottling company. He bought casks and bottled and sold them under his brand names Caledonian Selection, Spirit of the Isles and Celtic Legends, (which occasionally appear on auction sites), and his company name, Liquid Gold Enterprises Ltd, but still using the distillery name.

From 1996 to early 2000's he continued with this and was progressing reasonably well. For the first four years he was able to bottle almost anything he wanted, but at that time he didn't have the wherewithal to buy large parcels of casks. Larger independent companies such as Signatory, Gordon McPhail and Douglas Laing had better contacts in the industry for buying parcels of whisky and clearly more financial muscle. Anthony did not have that range or quality of contacts, but he was able to see from the interest in single casks, that this was changing people's perception of the malt whisky industry, which at that time was an industry dominated by seven or eight brands, pushing out age-statement single malts.

The independent bottlers wanted casks of the whiskies that had this recognition, but around the turn of the millennium, that tap was turned off, certainly to the smaller independent bottlers, who had real difficulty obtaining casks of Macallan, Highland Park, Laphroaig and the other premium brands of the time.

If he had wanted to carry on as an independent bottler, Anthony would have been buying secondary brands, as they were then, for which there was a limited immediately available market. He would have struggled to make a viable living on these scraps. How things have changed with many a sherried version of Auchroisk, Dailuaine, Ardmore and others being lapped up by a whisky-drinking public buying more with their eyes than their palates.

He needed to do something different and felt that to be able to control his, and his family's futures, he needed to control the supply, and to do this, he needed to build a distillery. A simple solution to a difficult problem – how hard could it be to build a distillery? He was going to find out and the next ten years would define whether he had a legacy or a failure, although I have come to realise from my discussions with Anthony that failure is not a word that appears in his vocabulary.

⊶⊷⋖◈⋗⊷⊶

Chapter 3

Realisation of a dream

Initially Anthony had considered purchasing the Glen Scotia distillery in Campbeltown. Kathy recalls that the scale was so massive, huge buildings that needed a significant amount of work and investment, that Anthony rejected that idea and then considered setting up his own distillery. He believed that the project to build Kilchoman would require significantly less money – he now laughs at his own naivety.

As Anthony quickly found out when he made further enquiries about establishing a new distillery, there were plenty of people who had similar ideas, but when they did the numbers, the idea quickly vanished into a six-year black hole, which would be the likely time from conception, through construction to the production of the first malt whisky after three years. There were also plenty of people, industry experts, friends and others who were quick to point out that he would be insane to open a distillery at that time.

Despite all the well-intentioned concern for his mental health, and perhaps because of some of the naysayers, Anthony was determined to push ahead with his vision, as he saw it in 2001. He was conscious that the last distillery built in Scotland was 1995 at Arran and prior to that it was the 60s or 70s, but those distilleries were generally built for blending purposes by the larger whisky producers. No new distilleries had been built on Islay in the preceding 120 years, but he was convinced that his idea was a sound one.

People questioned as there were over 100 distilleries in Scotland, that Anthony could build one which was likely to be any different to them. As there were also seven distilleries on Islay, they asked why the island needed another one. Anthony saw a growing demand and interest for single malt and felt that the time was right. Malt whisky was not just about producing 10, 15, 18-year-old malts, but was also about producing single casks, giving people variety and being prepared to do something different. If a malt whisky was good at three years old, then he wanted to break the shackles of market conformity and longstanding belief and sell a three-year-old whisky.

The new distillery was always going to be built on Islay. Firstly because of Kathy's family connections with the island and secondly, and quite specifically, was the Islay brand. Islay is synonymous with peated whiskies, and the tag line 'Islay Malt' conveys that to the would-be purchaser (accepting that there are unpeated whiskies made on Islay). He established the Kilchoman Distillery Company Ltd on 12 November 2001, in anticipation of raising the necessary funds to get the project off the ground.

Anthony professes that he didn't think too much about the money. He thought that he would have no issue raising the money to get the distillery built. How wrong he was! His initial views were that the costs would be in the region of £5m, in the end the costs were more than £10m and in reality, he should have budgeted for significantly more.

Kathy agrees that there were times during the process that she would quite happily have moved on from the venture, but Anthony never lost faith. She believed that he always considered it would work provided he could get the right investment. They had her grandfather's house on Islay that enabled them to release their own capital. She knew that Anthony felt that if they could create a new Islay malt whisky on a small scale at a farm-based distillery, then people would buy into that.

Anthony always believed that if he could get the distillery built, he could sell the whisky, with his 30 years' experience at the wholesale end of the drinks industry. The difficulty was trying to raise the money in the first instance, and he really struggled to raise £1m. It involved a lot of knocking on doors and attending meetings with potential investors, but no one was interested; it was too long term, too risky, all the issues facing any company looking to set up a new distillery at that time. Given the uncertainty in the whisky market, banks were very reluctant to get involved. Now, raising £20m for such an investment is considerably easier than raising £1m or even a fraction of that was, back in 2003.

Kilchoman was at the vanguard of the upsurge in whisky, and it was to be another fifteen years before that really manifested itself with significant growth across worldwide markets and the opening of many new Scottish distilleries.

Cash flow was a significant issue, and reasonable returns were 10-15 years away. Many distilleries now cover some early losses by producing gin and vodka, with its immediate turnaround and returns, as a precursor to the first whisky coming of age. Back in 2000, gin was very much the preserve of a limited number of producers and the gin revolution was still 15 years away.

In an interview with Gavin Smith of Whisky Magazine in 2002, Anthony said: **"I believe there is more and more interest in niche Scotch whisky products, and I think there's definitely room for a micro-distillery going right back to Scotch whisky's farming roots, with everything taking place on one site, from the growing of the barley to the maturing of the spirit. We have a number of private parties and whisky lovers from all over the world who have expressed an interest in investing in the project. Obviously, it's not a short-term investment, and Liquid Gold Enterprises will generate income to help offset a lot of the costs during the first seven years, before we have any whisky to sell. Kilchoman will be the most unique distillery in Scotland when it's up and running. All the output will be sold as single-cask bottlings, and nobody else is doing that."**

Anthony and Kathy had known the French family at Rockside Farm for many years. Their children were the same age, so the families did a lot together. Anthony and Mark had discussions when Anthony was considering building a distillery and his original intention was to build it on the Laggan Estate, where the family property was. The decision to ultimately build the distillery at Rockside Farm, Kilchoman was not an easy one. It was Mark's suggestion that he build the distillery at Rockside Farm, where there were existing farm buildings, which were unused and enough land to allow for a gentle expansion, when the time was right.

Whilst the romantic notion would be that the Macbeatha hypothesis (that whisky distillation was first brought over to the West Coast of Islay by the MacBeatha family from Northern Ireland, before heading over to the Scottish mainland), played heavily on Anthony's mind when considering location, the reality was that this was one of the best areas for growing barley on Islay, there was no other distillery close by and Mark French wanted to diversify.

Mark saw this as an additional income stream, which wouldn't have come from anywhere else, so an agreement was reached to rent the buildings from Mark and purchase an agreed amount of barley from him each year at a premium price, which was the input costs to Mark, with a 50% margin added on top. They didn't look at the market price as that could change artificially for other reasons.

Anthony wanted to have a farm distillery, as this had always been his aim. He needed to have a point of difference, otherwise it was just another distillery. Distillation on this small scale was how it was done 200 years earlier on Islay. He knew Mark French very well, so it made sense to rent the space from him.

Mark anticipated that due to the location there would be few visitors, the distillery would remain small and that he would be able to continue running his farm. He was getting additional income from the renting of the buildings and from the agreement to purchase barley. He was previously just growing feed barley, so he received an uplift in price, to that which he would normally have received. The buildings that were taken over were in the main not being used, so it was beneficial to both parties.

Anthony set out looking for individuals with £25,000 and above to invest (around late 2002/early 2003), but quickly found out that there were few individuals or companies that were prepared to put that sort of money in.

Henrik Aflodal represented a group of whisky aficionados from Sweden, about 50 altogether, who all put in a relatively small sum of money and became the Kilchoman Invest Group. These were individuals he knew from his previous life as an independent bottler.

Anthony approached landowners on Islay, most had already committed to supporting the resurgence of Bruichladdich and were unable to assist. Sir John Mactaggart, who owns an estate on Islay, had put a significant sum of money into the rebirth of Bruichladdich, indeed serving as Chairman of the Board of Bruichladdich from 2004-2012. In view of his investment in Bruichladdich, he was only able to put a small sum into Kilchoman. Timing, as in all areas of life, is everything.

Lord Margadale of Islay, was another landowner who was able to support in a limited financial way in the very early days. Harry Fitzalan Howard, a friend of Anthony also agreed to invest at the start of the venture. All these investors put money in, trusting the vision of one man, and probably not realising the sensible amount of money required to establish a distillery.

Claire Powell, was a friend of the French family, who owned Rockside Farm and Mr and Mrs Callum Rollo, who were friends of friends, heard about the venture and invested small sums.

Jonathan and Simon Turnbull, longstanding friends of Anthony, each invested at the start up, then subsequently put in significantly more funds through their business, at the time when the Kilchoman venture was in danger of failing. They were shareholders until around three years ago.

Mark French, was gifted shares, those shares being returned when Kilchoman bought the farm. He was initially a board member, but it was felt there was a conflict of interest as he was supplying barley and renting the buildings to the distillery, so he stepped down from the board.

As can be seen, despite Anthony's best efforts over a year or more, the various contributions at an early stage didn't amount to much more than £200,000. Anthony and his family then put in £500,000 (which was more money than they had), to enable the project to get off the ground at least. With the benefit of hindsight, Anthony realises that he shouldn't have given the go ahead at that stage to start construction as there was never going to be enough money to take him to profitability.

As he said to me, *"any sane person would have realised that £700,000 or so would not have got them very far."* It got him to the stage where he had built the distillery, and in his mind, if he built it, then people would come and buy his whisky. The reality was that much soul searching and fundraising would be necessary before the dream became a reality.

There was some financial support locally from the West of Scotland branch of the Bank of Scotland and from Highlands and Islands Enterprise for the build work. With their support Anthony had enough money to complete the initial build, but insufficient to meet running costs up until the time he was producing whisky.

When Anthony told his sons that they were going to move to Islay and build a distillery, they were a little nonplussed, as the full implication as to how this would change all their lives was not even in contemplation.

The buildings consisted of the old mill building, which because of its height was ideal to become the still house, one of the old stables was turned into the visitor centre and café and a steel portal framed building was erected for the first warehouse. There was a kiln and malting floor, mill, mash tun, four washbacks, wash still and spirit still, with a single warehouse and a café/visitor centre.

Whilst undertaking the onerous task of raising money to build the distillery, Anthony was also looking at the style of whisky he wanted to produce. Charlie Maclean MBE, a critically acclaimed whisky writer and one of the most respected men in the whisky world had been a friend of Anthony's for many years. Anthony rang him early in 2003 and asked if he had to pick one person that could guide him through production and achieving a particular style of spirit, who would it be? Charlie said that there was only one person for the task and that was Jim Swan. Dr Jim Swan was hugely instrumental in setting the parameters for the Kilchoman spirit and assisting with the initial cask choices.

2003 was around the time that Jim had established his own consultancy. He had a PhD in Chemistry and Biological Sciences from Heriot-Watt University, was a Fellow of the Royal Society of Chemistry and was subsequently awarded Fellowship of the Institute of Brewing and Distilling. He had written many scientific papers and was a judge at the International Wine and Spirits Competition. He had also assisted Penderyn, when they initially set up in 2000 and many distilleries since then.

Discussions took place with Jim, and Anthony explained what he was trying to achieve; a soft, fruity, clean, peated spirit, which would work well with different cask types and that they could bottle at a younger age. Jim then went away and produced the design for the stills, and indicated whilst the Oregon Pine washbacks might look better, from a practical perspective stainless steel ones were cheaper and much easier to clean. As the distillery was on the west coast of Islay, in a temperate climate, there was less need for the wooden washbacks (as would often be used in the Highlands) to retain heat. Since installation, they have not had any issues, the washbacks work well and came cheaper than pine washbacks.

As Anthony had no experience at producing whisky, he took Jim Swan at face value and accepted all his recommendations. He described Jim as an incredibly humble man, a scientist, who went about things in a quiet manner, but his results at several distilleries suggest that he was certainly the right man to advise Anthony. Many other consultants may have been distillery managers and understood the process of distilling, but Jim understood it on a micro-biological level, because of his in-depth background in chemistry.

Jim was a delightful person to work with, according to Anthony and his three sons. He never tried to baffle Anthony or the boys with science, he would explain in layman's terms how he was going to make something happen.

There was an initial meeting with Jim and discussions regarding the style of whisky and specifically what Anthony hoped to achieve, and how many litres of alcohol per year he was looking to produce. Anthony then approached John McDougall, (who had previously worked at Laphroaig and was Distillery Manager at Springbank for 10 years), with a clear notion of the type of distillery he wanted and the traditional Islay style of spirit he wanted it to produce.

Ron Gibson, a chemical engineer who ran Carrick Technical Services Ltd in Girvan, Ayrshire, was recruited to assist John McDougall. Ultimately Ron took over from John and completed the overall design of the distillery layout. He put together the drawings, showing where all the equipment would go and how it would fit into the available space. He remained working with Anthony until everything was initially fitted. Ron previously worked for William Grant & Sons Ltd and was responsible for the design and construction of their Kininvie Distillery in Dufftown.

Choice of contractor when first constructing the distillery was very important to Anthony. He wanted to go with a local contractor. Woodrow Construction were known to Anthony before they became involved in the construction of the distillery, as Arthur Woodrow had done work for Kathy's father at his house. Anthony knew he had a good team around him, so they were the natural choice.

Arthur Woodrow, who is sadly no longer with us, is described by Anthony as an 'old school gentleman'. He recognised part way through construction of the distillery that Anthony was struggling to pay, but he finished the job for Anthony, and he was paid the balance three years later. He said to Anthony that he had been through similar cash flow issues himself and that Anthony should pay him when he could. Without the generosity of Arthur Woodrow, the project may not even have been completed. The distillery continued working with Woodrow Construction until Arthur died, and the company was dissolved in 2013.

Forsyths Ltd was commissioned to manufacture and install the distilling equipment but when Anthony received the turnkey quote from

Richard Forsyth, he thought it was expensive (bearing in mind the tight finances) so he decided to use other contractors (not Woodrows) to do the pipe work and install a second-hand boiler, which he concedes was a mistake. Forsyths completed all the electrics.

Once installed and commissioned, he discovered that the pipes from the boiler were of an insufficient bore, meaning that steam couldn't be delivered to the stills at the correct temperature. The contractors he had chosen had limited experience of this type of installation, which was presumably why they were cheaper. Anthony had to get Forsyths back to replace the pipework and he bought a new boiler. As with many other matters at the distillery, this was a lesson learnt, and subsequently, whenever there is any significant work to be done at the distillery, it is put in the hand of a single contractor, who is responsible for managing the trades and therefore managing the timing of the works.

Anthony wanted Kathy to design the visitor centre and café. Kathy's sister, Nicola Wilks, is an interior designer, and she came in and helped with the design specifically of the visitor centre, which was dark with only a window at one end, so designing something appealing was key. With the limited funds that she was given, Nicola did a terrific job, bringing light and warmth into the café and shop.

In April 2005, following an advert placed in the Ileach newspaper, Malcolm Rennie was appointed the first Distillery Manager. Malcolm was the son of a cooper, whose family moved to Islay in the early 1970s, originally to Bunnahabhain. He joined Ardbeg as a Stillman in 1997 after a stint in the merchant navy. Whilst working for Glenmorangie, he spent some time as Assistant Manager at Glen Moray. He wanted to take a step up and became Anthony's first Distillery Manager. He stayed with Kilchoman until 2010, when he left to help set up Annandale in the Borders. More recently he was appointed as Distillery Manager at Rosebank. You will see his signature on the early bottles of Kilchoman, alongside Anthony's.

By the start of June and 2005 Fèis, the distillery was still being completed. The stillhouse installation and the malting floor were complete, although the kiln and warehouse No. 1 were still under construction. It was intended that the first spirit would be distilled during Fèis week, but that clearly couldn't happen as they were behind with the build. Anthony took the view that he would officially open at the Fèis and the first warehouse tours were undertaken. Paula Lawson started her job as the first Visitor Centre Manager in April and with Kathy and a small team, ensured the visitor centre café was open at the festival.

In those early days, Kathy and Anthony had a friend who had run pubs, and she helped them set up the menu for the café, the formula for which they have maintained since opening the distillery to the present day. It produces very little wastage and provides good simple food, which generally is what people want when visiting a distillery.

In the early days of the café, Kathy struggled to employ anyone locally and they desperately wanted to open to showcase the distillery and to create a café where people would want to come. Visitors to the distillery were key to its success.

Kathy went to an agency and employed two Polish girls, one who worked for a single season and the other for two seasons, both fully committing themselves to the business. This enabled them to build up a reputation and they were then able to recruit locally. Kathy worked six days in the café, of the seven that they were open. This was seen very simply as an additional revenue stream, at a time when revenue was very limited.

Following on from the festival, the remaining building work was completed, and the first seven refill bourbon casks were filled on 14 December 2005. No more casks were then filled until the following March. Four years after the conception of an idea, the realisation of that dream had come to fruition. Following on from that dream was the harsh reality over the next four years of having no money and being close to despair on many occasions.

⸻◆◇◆⸻

Chapter 4

Knights in shining armour

There is little doubt that without further significant investment over the period 2006-2009, the business would have failed. Anthony had just about enough money to get the distillery built, but going forward there was insufficient money to pay wages, buy barley and deal with all day to day running costs of the distillery.

In the early days to assist cashflow, the business sold over 300 casks, which was the right thing to do at the time, at £950 and £1000 each. Kilchoman stopped selling casks mid-2007. The board made the decision that they couldn't continue selling casks otherwise they would not have their own whisky to sell. Anthony's view was that if they wanted to develop a brand, then they would regret selling too many of those casks, unless they were producing such a quantity that this represented only a small proportion, which at that time, it did not. The lack of early casks has been evident in recent years as Kilchoman has been trying to buy back casks from the original owners, with limited success.

With only 50,000 litres of spirit produced in 2006, consisting of 326 Bourbon Barrels, 23 Fresh Oloroso Sherry Butts and 4 Fresh Oloroso Sherry Hogsheads, the casks sold to individuals represented most of that year's production, so Anthony was right to be cautious.

In his early dealings with Jim Swan, it was plain to Anthony that one of Jim's areas of greatest expertise was cask maturation. He is well known for his development of the STR (shaved, toasted and recharred) cask, initially using Portuguese wine casks, which he developed in co-operation with the J. Dias Cooperage in Porto, Portugal. The STR cask was born out of the need for more casks to mature single malt, and an abundance of wine casks across Europe and America.

All Anthony's contacts for cask supply came from Jim Swan in those early days, and he still uses the same contacts now. Kilchoman went to Speyside Cooperage for the first year of operation like many other distilleries.

From there he knew he would always get good quality casks, but from a wide range of bourbon houses, so the consistency of flavour would not be there.

Kilchoman had to use Speyside during that first year, as they were not yet established and Buffalo Trace, owned by Sazarac, would not work with Kilchoman as they were too small, and had no reputation. With the assistance of Jim Swan, Kilchoman secured a contract towards the end of 2006, which has been uninterrupted until 2023, when Sazarac started keeping their casks within their business and Kilchoman moved to the Breckenridge Distillery in Colorado, which incidentally is the highest whisky (whiskey) distillery in the world.

Bodega José y Miguel Martin agreed to supply Kilchoman with sherry casks, which resulted partly from the involvement of Jim Swan. Anthony recalls that he contacted Glenfarclas during the early days of establishing Kilchoman and asked them, where they sourced their casks from. He was told Bodega José y Miguel Martin, and immediately contacted them, and arrangements were made to supply Kilchoman with the requisite casks. Their strong relationship has continued to this day. Anthony has been out to Spain with Kathy a few times and had met on each occasion with Miguel, whom he describes as *"a delightful man, deeply passionate in his quest to produce the finest quality sherry."*

Jim Swan's legacy is a simple one. A consistent character of spirit, placed into the best quality casks, sampled on a regular basis, allows the production of consistently high-quality malt whisky. Anthony has experimented a little with yeast varieties and cut points on the spirit over time, but basically the Jim Swan mantra lives on at Kilchoman and will remain at the heart of everything that they do.

Kilchoman was always destined to be a premium whisky and therefore required premium branding. Anthony owned a company called Caledonian Selection prior to establishing Kilchoman and Craig Mackinlay had worked with Anthony at that time designing some single cask labels. Anthony approached Craig and asked him if he could design a brand logo for Kilchoman. That would have been around 2003/2004 when he was putting together his business plan.

At that time, Craig was Head of Design for an agency in Glasgow (he established his own business Breeze Creative Design Consultants around 20 years ago). He put forward three or four designs for discussion. Anthony wanted just a nod to Islay and its Celtic origins, but not a full Celtic design, as seen in the Ardbeg logo. That is why the 'h' of Kilchoman has that Celtic swirl on the leg (I must confess that until I spoke with Craig, I had never noticed there was a Celtic device at the foot of the 'h').

There is always a 'secondary device' in the designs that Craig creates and that is seen on the shoulder of the bottle, with the roundel that says 'Uniquely Islay' with again the Celtic device.

From late 2005 to 2008 Kilchoman was bottling new make spirit and spirit that could not yet be called whisky, as it was not three years old. Craig designed the packaging for the miniature sets although the initial production runs used an 'off the shelf' bottle from Saverglass in France.

After all the delays and issues suffered in the build-up, just as the distillery seemed to be up and running, on February 12, 2006, there was a fire in the kiln. Kilchoman at the time were using anthracite as the fuel to dry the barley (anthracite burns very hot and goes very cold quickly). Peter and Anthony stacked up the anthracite as they were going away to watch the England v Scotland rugby match at their farmhouse in Laggan, around 10 miles away. They stacked the anthracite too high; it burned very hot, and the kiln caught fire. They were contacted by the French family to let them know the kiln was on fire.

There is apparently a way of telling if the malt is on fire, as it smells of Horlicks (I am sure that other malty drinks would have a similar smell) and this would have been obvious in the locality, however, the French family only contacted them when they saw flames coming out of the kiln, where they shouldn't have been. Thankfully, the fire was prevented from spreading to other buildings.

Whilst it was not possible to malt their own barley for several months, the Port Ellen Maltings was able to meet their malt demands at 50ppm until the beginning of 2008. The idea of producing all malt in-house was abandoned at this time and two separate product lines were subsequently created: 100% Islay, made from barley malted to approximately 20 ppm, where Kilchoman carries out all aspects of production itself i.e. from growing the barley to bottling the whisky, and all other bottlings, which would use Port Ellen malt at 50ppm, albeit the rest of the production would take place at Kilchoman.

Throughout 2006 and into 2007, Anthony was fighting to keep the distillery open. The boys helped as best they could during the holidays from school and university with endless rounds of painting, labouring, and doing whatever jobs were necessary.

Once they had sufficient staff in place in the café, Kathy moved into the offices and helped more with the administration of the business. Kathy was Company Secretary during those early days, albeit not entirely sure of everything that entailed, but she did meet with HMRC whenever they came over to Islay. When they started shipping goods abroad, Kathy was more involved on the Customs side of things, ensuring there were no hold ups. She admits that they made a lot of mistakes during those early years, because they had so little experience to draw upon.

They do say that fortune favours the brave and completely by chance in summer 2006, Niels Ladefoged came through the door of the distillery. Niels had friends who lived on Islay, his daughter wanted to go riding and they had facilities at the farm. Whilst his daughter was riding, Niels came into the distillery and chatted with Anthony, who by now was desperate to get additional funding. Niels went away and spoke with Moonpal Singh Grewal, a businessman holding Domino Pizza franchises, amongst other businesses and they initially made quite a modest investment.

At around the same time, again quite by chance, Dr John Thorogood, who at the time was employed in the oil industry had flown down to Islay for a holiday. He came down the track to the farm as he heard there was a farm shop. When he reached the end of the track, he realised there was no farm shop, but there was a distillery on site. He had a discussion with Anthony at that stage, who said that he was still looking for investors and he agreed to invest, what at that time was a significant sum.

As 2007 wore on, with the continuing weekly costs and the lack of cash investment meant that the business was on its knees, Niels and Moonpal offered to invest a large amount of money, sufficient to get over the issues at that time. This would come at a significant cost to Anthony, as the dilution in his own family's shareholding would have been such that he was no longer incentivised in working to the extent that he had been, so he turned them down. The Wills family were originally 75% owners of the business and risked dilution down to around 10%, which was unpalatable to Anthony.

At this time, Anthony was also talking to two retired ex-Diageo executives, but that again came to nothing. The bank continued to be supportive, up to a point, by extending deadlines. The Turnbulls had committed their further investment earlier in the year and John Thorogood had also made a further investment. The feeling seemed to be that they had come this far, and a further investment might just see Kilchoman through to profitability. They did make it clear that this was not a bottomless pit and there would come a point, despite their friendship, where the Turnbulls would say, "no more."

Despite knocking on a lot of doors, there were no more obvious investors in the wings and the Turnbulls suggested to Anthony that he needed to go back to Niels and Moonpal, but with a deal that meant he was incentivised to keep working in the business.

When he phoned Niels, it was with a degree of trepidation that Anthony put forward his counter offer. Niels accepted that it was beneficial to all shareholders that Anthony was incentivised to stay working in the business. The agreement meant that Niels and Moonpal had a significantly increased stake, whilst Anthony's stake was reduced to 19%. There were also background discussions to which Anthony was not privy, between the Turnbulls and Niels/Moonpal, which undoubtedly helped to conclude this deal. The alternative was that the business would fail and that was something which was not in the best interests of any of the parties.

When the Turnbulls initially invested, they had a financial director, who came up and reviewed the books and the overall operation, with a completely dispassionate eye. He stayed with the Wills family for a few days, and apart from Anthony putting him in a bedroom where the heating wasn't on and there were no sheets on the bed, it was a very worthwhile visit. He reported that the business just needed some money to cover the next couple of years and then it should be profitable. It provided confidence to the Turnbulls to continue supporting the business, at a time when their involvement was crucial.

The distillery continued to operate. In May 2008 a new website was launched and at the Kilchoman Open Day of Fèis 2008, Jim Swan presented a 'Spirit Tasting with New Make', a one-year-old and a two-year-old Kilchoman, the first indications of the type of product we were ultimately likely to taste.

Bramble Liqueur was also launched at the Fèis. This was a liqueur made from blackberries and honey macerated with Kilchoman New Make, providing strong peat smoke and fruity sweetness. This was an excellent product, selling well until it was stopped in 2022.

Kathy recalls in the earliest days going to shows with new make spirit, or 'In Anticipation' two-year-old spirit to show people what their ultimate whisky might be like. She didn't go on many trips with Anthony but does recall one trip to New Zealand. They received a lot of supportive feedback from those early days, making invaluable contacts. Now with the boys going to shows it has a similar impact, with customers and distributors being impressed with the family commitment to their markets, rather than just using anonymous salespeople, who have no real affinity with the brand. Kilchoman employ talented salespeople, who work alongside the family and who all care passionately about the brand, but ultimately the family legacy is key to Kilchoman's success.

In Autumn 2008, Kilchoman distillate matured for two years in bourbon casks was produced in the first of a series of 12 single cask bottlings over 2008 and 2009. As this product was not three years old, it could not be called whisky. Later in 2008 Kilchoman sold a presentation box with three 5cl miniature bottles of Kilchoman Spirit under the title 'The Connoisseurs Pack: one month, one year and two years old'. This was to bring in revenue at a critical phase in the survival of the business, but it also showcased the light and sweet nature of the spirit, an indicator of what it might become.

The barley harvest at Rockside Farm in 2008 yielded 100 tonnes. By the time of the Christmas shutdown, Kilchoman reported an annual production of 91,500 lpa. Apart from a production stoppage in June due to severe drought, during which repairs were also carried out on the boiler, production was maintained throughout the year.

One of the issues with the business during late 2006, 2007 and the first part of 2008, was that Anthony spent all his time firefighting, trying to bring in more money, eke out the money that they had and make do and mend the equipment they had. This substantial cash injection, whilst diluting his personal stake in the business, ensured that they would get the business through to selling whisky and that is where he could now put all his focus.

There was a need for a further cash injection to aid expansion and following the banking crisis of 2008, this was never going to come from the banks, so loans were given to the business in 2009 by the Turnbulls, John Thorogood and Niels/Moonpal amounting to around £1.5m, with appropriate repayment terms. They discussed this away from Anthony, and rather than dilute Anthony's share of the business further, recognising that he was essential to the brand, these were presented as loans, which were appropriately timetabled for repayment. The money was repaid within two years. The business has been self-funding ever since.

A crisis had been averted by astute businessmen recognising that the distillery needed finance, but to dilute its founder to such an extent that he was disincentivised was neither prudent nor financially astute. The loan of money to the business at that time, on appropriate terms was precisely the right way of ensuring that everyone's interests were aligned, and the money was available to allow the business to expand.

It was around 2008 that a German vet, Hans-Peter Neumann and his wife Berit, first came to Kilchoman, having followed the story and development of the distillery. Hans-Peter and Berit have been travelling to Scotland and particularly Islay, with a love of malt whisky for 30 years.

They tasted the whisky when it was first rolled out as a three-year-old in 2009 and considered it was a beautifully balanced whisky for one so young. Although they didn't buy any casks at that time, as they were too late, they did buy some later from Alba, the company that was distributing Kilchoman at that time. This included Cask No5 of 2006, a refill bourbon cask, one of the very early casks filled at the distillery. Hans-Peter is probably the biggest Kilchoman collector in the world, with over 800 bottles.

He was part of a group of German friends, who travelled together to Scotland, to whisky fairs and events. They met up in 2008 or 2009 on the island of Rugen in Germany and agreed that they wanted to establish a website, which followed the fortunes of one of the whiskies they all loved, so Kilchomania (www.kilchomania.com) was born.

Alongside the web pages following the events at the distillery, they wanted to establish a database, detailing all the whiskies issued by Kilchoman, from the earliest times. Many international friends assist with input on single cask bottlings in other jurisdictions and often help Hans-Peter obtain these bottles. The core 'club' for Kilchomania consists of no more than 10 people now and Hans-Peter is the only writer of the content.

Such is the accuracy of the database, which is not held by Kilchoman themselves, that the management team at Kilchoman will refer new starters to the database and website to understand the history of the business and the bottles they produce.

❖

Chapter 5

The development of a brand

There was clearly a developing interest in the brand, as in May 2009 at the Fèis, Anthony Wills auctioned for charity a single bottle of whisky taken from the first cask (Distilled on 14/12/2005, bottled on 22/5/2009 @60.7%), which was sold for £5,400. Interestingly a second bottle raised £7,000 in 2015 for the Beatson Cancer charity and in 2023 a third bottle from this cask was sold for £15,000 by Sotheby's for the Distillers One of One charitable effort to raise money for The Youth Action Fund in Scotland.

090909 is a very significant number within the Wills Household and in the Kilchoman story, as on 09 September 2009, Kilchoman Distillery released its first whisky, and following a great deal of discussion, handwringing and with a spark of marketing genius, they came up with the label 'Inaugural Release'.

This whisky epitomised the style that Anthony wanted to produce, a light fruity peated dram. It spent three years in fresh ex-bourbon barrels and was then finished for five months in Oloroso sherry butts. As part of the joy of drinking whisky is its varied appearance, it was not coloured in any way and as Kilchoman will always be presented at least 46% ABV or above, it is non-chill filtered. 8,450 bottles of this historic fluid were produced, and I daresay that many still lie undisturbed in private collections.

Kathy remembers the launch party for their inaugural release, and Richard Forsyth was talking to another guest and said that Anthony was the only distiller he knew (at that time) who had been out in the wild selling the promise of a whisky, that was still two or three years away from being produced. Anthony effectively created a market for his whisky well before it was even on the shelves – now it is commonplace to see new make spirit being a regular feature in distillery sales.

Anthony had spent a lot of time away from home during those early years, the production side was set up but there were still maintenance issues and selling the promise of whisky down the line was all-consuming. The fact that Anthony saw the need to sell the whisky well in advance of making it, was probably what saved the business, and he was to continue travelling widely, selling the brand for some years, until his sons took on the mantle.

From 10 September, the Inaugural Edition was available in 14 countries worldwide, mainly Europe at this stage with Canada, New Zealand and Japan, as the US and other Far eastern markets had not yet been established. The whisky was received exceptionally well throughout its markets and sold out at £45 within a day, so the brand was being established very quickly.

Six days after the Inaugural Release, La Maison du Whisky (LMDW) in Paris released the first bottling of a Kilchoman single cask, which was a Bourbon Barrel 232/2006, again receiving critical acclaim in France.

This resulted in distributors ringing up and emailing Anthony, saying that they wanted to represent the distillery in various regions. There were no plans in the early days to go into any specific market, it was merely a question of getting the whisky produced. There was some media interest at the time of construction, but Anthony didn't need to get on a plane looking for distributors, they came to him. He used his contacts within the trade, and through other distillers and asked about particular retailers. He had also grown some contacts himself through whisky fairs and meets in different parts of the world and such is the whisky industry, they were only too happy to provide advice and assistance.

In 2009 there were 14 markets, including the UK into which the Inaugural Release was sold, who perhaps took 20 cases each and the remainder was sold through the distillery. From the earliest time they had 14 export markets to work into.

November 2009 saw the second Kilchoman release, which was intended as the first of a series of seasonal releases. Autumn 2009 Release was to be followed by four further releases in the series, until Spring 2011. This was matured in Bourbon barrels for three years and finished in Oloroso Sherry Butts for two and a half months. There were 10,000 bottles sold in 15 countries worldwide and for this distribution, Taiwan was added as a new market.

As much as Jim Swan was responsible for developing the type of spirit and the quality of casks used at the distillery during the early years, others also had a major impact on the way in which the Kilchoman brand was developed and none more so than John Maclellan, who took over from Malcolm Rennie as Distillery Manager in May 2010.

John started his distillery life at Bunnahabhain as a Mashman in March 1989. He became a brewer at the distillery in 1995, developing his skills and broadening his understanding of the whisky industry. Two years later he was appointed Distillery Manager, and according to those around at the time, his natural good humour and disarming way with people, made him a perfect fit.

As manager at Bunnahabhain, John was responsible for establishing the annual Fèis Ìle bottling, which all other distilleries on the island subsequently adopted. He was also responsible for the relaunch of the Bunnahabhain single malt.

By 2010, with the family growing up and moving on, he was keen for a change in direction. His appointment as general manager at Kilchoman Distillery was a new, much longed-for challenge.

He was instrumental in helping to launch Kilchoman's flagship expressions, the 100% Islay in 2011 and Machir Bay in 2012, and took enormous pride when they both won medals at the prestigious International Wine and Spirits Competition. In 2013 he was voted joint Distillery Manager of the Year by the Whisky Magazine, in recognition of his work at Kilchoman.

His cancer diagnosis in early 2014, at the age of 58, was a crushing blow, but one he faced with typical resolve. His death was a significant loss to the whisky industry and an even greater loss to his loved ones.

Tributes paid to John from work and industry colleagues at the time, were that he was *'charismatic'*, *'warm hearted'*, *'one of Islay's best'*, *'a true gentleman'* and *'one of the greatest men the whisky industry has ever known'*.

By the time of the 'Spring 2010 Release' the distribution was to 19 countries worldwide, with Australia, Hong Kong and Japan being added to the countries outside of Europe.

In August 2010, due to the increasing demand worldwide for Kilchoman, they proposed to increase production over the winter months, as there would be no issue with water supply then. To assist, they hired a third member of the production team, Robin Bignal, initially on a part-time basis. Robin so impressed with his work on the production team that he eventually became Production Manager and has worked closely with Anthony in more recent years on cask selection and vatting. His knowledge of casks and where they are located within the growing number of warehouses is encyclopaedic.

At the Kilchoman Open Day of Fèis 2010, the distillery released its first Fèis Ìle bottling, a single bourbon cask exactly three years old. Fèis is seen as a showcase for all that is good about a distillery, so great care is taken every year to ensure a bottling which is different to previous years, but which shows the interested public exactly what the distillery is capable of.

In August 2010 the Summer Release was the 4th edition of the Seasonal Releases. By this time, they were exporting to the USA, which represented a massive step for Kilchoman, with a further market of 340m people. This was followed with two single cask releases for the USA, produced as part of a promotional tour that Anthony undertook in late 2010.

During 2010 approximately 100,000 litres of alcohol were produced and 50,000 bottles of Kilchoman whisky were sold.

In March 2011 the sixth and final of the quarterly seasons bottlings was released called the 'Spring 2011 Release'. Anthony had plans for standard releases going forward.

April saw the introduction of a Distillery only release for the first time, purchased at the visitor centre. These releases have proved popular and are available to the present day. At this time there were a lot of single cask bottlings as Kilchoman was trying to make its name in a wide range of markets. A single cask bottled a few days earlier for Denmark, became the first five-year-old Kilchoman whisky, and this distillery bottling was the second.

At the beginning of June, a new bottling room was completed, representing a massive change for the distillery. Prior to this they were bottling single casks or small batches, with hand-written labels.

The Heath Robinson method previously employed to fill casks involved the filling of a clean plastic dustbin with whisky, which was filtered by hand and the bottles filled with a teapot. The teapot happened to be exactly the right size to fill a single bottle – 70cl. Unfortunately, anything for the USA market needed a top up, with bottles being 75cl! Oh, the joys of running a farm distillery! Anthony used to sit with John Maclellan on the old malt floor, filling the bottles by hand of an evening and labelling them. It was a time when everyone put in whatever hours were necessary to make this dream work, often late into the evening.

Anthony knew Simon Coughlin and Mark Rainier at Bruichladdich and they allowed Kilchoman to use their bottling kit for what was a couple of years, prior to installing the new bottling line. When Kilchoman produced their first single malt in 2009, they had to take the whisky down to 46%, and they produced over 8,000 bottles in that release, so it would have been impossible to fill the bottles using the teapot method.

Bruichladdich had a semi-automatic four-head vacuum filler, which was hardly used, as they had moved on in terms of their own production. Kilchoman took an IBC down to Bruichladdich with bottles and corks and returned with filled bottles, ready for labelling. At this time, they had a semi-automatic capping machine, but still had to put on all the corks by hand, there was a single label machine, where the bottle was inserted and the label adhered, still very labour intensive. The new bottling line saved a great deal of time and effort.

This system ran for around two years, when they extended the line, in the same room, running the bottling round in a semi-circle.

The kindness showed by Bruichladdich was typical of the support that distilleries provide to each other on Islay and Anthony is immensely grateful to Simon and Mark for their support.

Kilchoman is one of only a few distilleries that produce single casks. It is problematic to set up the bottling plant and labelling machines to do single casks, hence why many distilleries shy away from them. Many distilleries are automated and not set up to produce single casks, as the downtime would be crippling. Kilchoman see this as one of their key differentiators. They will produce single casks for key distributors, for regions, or for the distillery shop.

It was also at this time in 2011 that Kilchoman introduced the Craig Mackinlay designed bottle with a thick glass base, larger corks and the Kilchoman 'coin' glued on, which is still used today. As they had large stocks of the older style bottle in 75cl for the US market these continued to be used for the next two years.

June 2011 saw the production of the first annual release, the aptly named '100% Islay Inaugural Release'. This was the fulfilment of a dream from nearly ten years earlier for Anthony, a whisky wholly produced on the farm. The barley had been grown there, malting, kilning, mashing, fermenting, distilling, and bottling had all been carried out on site. 'From barley to bottle' was the inevitably adopted slogan, one which only a handful of distilleries can boast of. This release was a vatting of over three-year-old fresh and refill Bourbon barrels.

To keep the momentum, in November 2011 the 'Vintage 2006' was introduced with whisky distilled in 2006. It was the intention, in the future, that a new edition was to be released every two years, each of which would have one more year storage time, so Vintage 2007 would be six years old and so on.

2012, was another breakthrough year for Kilchoman, with the production of the first of its real core range products (100% Islay was to be an annual production, but with a limited release of bottles). Machir Bay 2012 was intended to be permanently available in all Kilchoman markets. As with many of the subsequently produced whiskies, this edition is named after one of Islay's most beautiful West coast locations, this being a glorious, usually empty bay with acres of golden sand. Bottled in batches, there was an intention to increase the age of the whiskies as more aged stock became available.

This first release was a vatting of three, four and five-year-old first fill ex-bourbon barrels, with the four-year old casks being finished in Oloroso sherry butts for eight weeks. These bottles were available from 01 March 2012 bottles at around £38.50 from the distillery, through its website and through retailers worldwide. The initial bottling sold very well and was extremely well received around the world. Anthony is aware that pricing is one of the key elements of product development. Machir Bay is priced where it is not the cheapest, but as it is still sub-£50 11 years later, it remains within the premium, but affordable malt whisky range.

Whilst the distillery had been producing the limited releases, they needed a core expression, which was available all the time. Distributors wanted something that they could permanently list. Anthony's view was that it was impossible to grow a brand by issuing small batch releases, and that Kilchoman needed core products, Machir Bay being the first of these. First year sales were around 15,000 bottles, which for a new release was excellent. The growth of Machir Bay over the following ten years has been very significant, with sales now approaching 200,000 bottles.

In April 2012 the first sherry cask release, limited to 6,000 bottles, was introduced to the market. The whisky was matured for four and a half years in Oloroso sherry butts. In the future Kilchoman would bring out a Sherry

Cask Release every year, but it was not until the second release in 2013 that it was named 'Loch Gorm'.

Anthony had always intended to have a minimum of two core expressions, which became Machir Bay and Sanaig, two regular limited annual expressions, which would be 100% Islay and Loch Gorm, together with possibly two other limited expressions, changing annually. In addition to this, single casks and batches would be produced for targeted markets or for sale through the distillery. Having that mix of different products with different price points, allows the company to create a greater margin. Many companies have their core range and produce nothing else, but then, many of those already have 100+ years of history to call on.

Charity is very much at the heart of the distillery, with an intention to support local projects, where possible. Kilchoman has sponsored the Islay Pipe band since 2012, the Distillery producing a single cask bottling for several years to provide funds for the band. They have also sponsored the Machrie Open golf tournament in May for many years and for four years sponsored the beach rugby which their team won in 2012. Kilchoman donated the proceeds of a cask to the WW100 Islay charity in recognition of the nearly 700 sailors of the SS Tuscania and HMS Otranto, who lost their lives in separate tragic sinkings in 1918.

In July 2012 Kilchoman established a new website and this coincided with the launch of the Kilchoman Club. The Club intended to report on distillery news and in common with other similar distilleries, offer an annual bottling. The first bottling for the Kilchoman Club was released in October 2012.

The Club, in keeping with similar offerings from other distilleries has proved very popular, especially amongst those that might not be able to travel to Islay, but it still provides them with an opportunity to purchase an annual bottle.

In August, due to a breakdown of the kiln, Kilchoman produced 'unpeated' whisky from the farm's own barley, for a very short period, filling 75 casks. As the low wines and feints receiver was not emptied between distillation runs with peated malt from Port Ellen, the result was a whisky with a slight peat smoke note, which is why Kilchoman refers to it as 'unpeated', to differentiate it from the 20 or 50ppm malts.

Anthony recognised that there was a need to produce more whisky, sales were very good, and stocks were getting low. To meet the ever-increasing demand for storage, Kilchoman started construction of a new warehouse complex in Conisby, on the other side of the Rhinns on Loch Indaal in August 2012. Warehouse No. 1 on the distillery site had been full for some time and Kilchoman had been forced to store some of its casks in other warehouses, on the island. There was capacity for 10,000 casks in two connected warehouses.

In 2012 the distillery produced 124,719 litres of pure alcohol and filled 844 casks.

Chapter 6

Relationships

It is Kilchoman's relationships with their distributors and importers, which has driven the business forward, almost since the inception of the business. One of the most important of those relationships is the one that Anthony developed with Sam Filmus at ImpEx Beverages in California, simply because of the size of the US market, with 340m citizens, all potential customers at present or sometime in the future.

The relationship started around 2009/10. John Hansell creator of the Malt Advocate and a beer and whisky writer in the USA recommended Impex Beverages to Anthony. Sam Filmus subsequently received a call from Anthony, who advised that he was coming to the USA and was looking for a US importer/distributor. Sam had been watching the development of Kilchoman since its earliest days and was intrigued by what the distillery had to offer.

Sam and his family founded JVS Imports over 20 years ago importing and distributing wines from Eastern Europe. This business expanded to importing spirits and beers across the spectrum. ImpEx Beverages was founded by Sam in 2008 in California as an importer of spirits, initially focussing on Scotch whisky, so at the time it seemed to be the perfect fit for Kilchoman.

ImpEx made a conscious decision in its infancy to only take one malt whisky from each of the regions of Scotland, to allow for greater focus and they were looking for an Islay whisky to add to this portfolio. Anthony arrived just at the right time for Sam and ImpEx and the two men hit it off immediately, with their passion for premium whisky and so began a business and personal friendship, which has endured for 14 years. It was also a great opportunity for ImpEx to progress with Kilchoman as the distillery developed its reputation, due in no small part to the assistance of distributors such as ImpEx.

Sam recalls the first whisky arriving in the USA in 2010, which was the Inaugural Release, in the old-style bottle. He had seen the new bottles available in Europe and asked Anthony when they were going to get these in the USA, Anthony replied that they could have them when they had sold 1000 cases. This was achieved in a short space of time and Sam received his new style bottles.

Impex started to promote the Kilchoman whisky, initially a big challenge as this NAS whisky (in essence three or four years old) was being sold at a similar price point to established ten-year-old and sixteen-year-old Islay whiskies (names withheld to protect the other distilleries!).

Over the years ImpEx has presented at hundreds of tastings, demos, trade and distributor events, promoting Kilchoman and the other brands that it imports. Few had heard of Kilchoman in the early days. This changed dramatically over the years, as now Sam believes that nine out of ten people at events that ImpEx attends have heard of Kilchoman, which is a testament to the work done in the USA by Sam and his team and the wider marketing by the Kilchoman team.

Whilst Sam and Anthony do not agree on everything, on important matters they quickly reach consensus. Specifically on the consistent pricing of whisky worldwide, both see the importance of not inflating prices in certain markets. This is especially true in the USA, where different states have different excise taxes and margins. Sam sees his relationship with Anthony as that of partners, where they can put their heads together and find solutions to some of the unique problems found in the USA.

The USA has 48 states which currently take Kilchoman, but dealing with them on occasion is like dealing with 48 different countries according to Sam. Seventeen US states are control states, where the government acts as the wholesaler. In these control states, Kilchoman is supplied on a 'special order' basis, which makes matters more complicated for Sam and his team.

Some states are franchise states, where the use of distributors is enshrined in State franchise laws, such that, where they exist, they provide an in-state distributor with assurance that they will not be abruptly terminated by their suppliers for no reason. It is therefore essential in those states that ImpEx select at the outset the best state distributor, who will support and promote the brand and create as few issues for ImpEx as possible.

I mention these issues in the USA, as it was essential for Anthony that he paired with the best importer, someone who would promote the brand, and would deal with the multitude of internal state issues, problems which are unique to the USA. He could have picked an individual importer/distributor in all the key states, but it made much more sense to appoint one distributor with his finger on the pulse of all states. Anthony had neither the time nor the inclination to pick up these issues from the North-West coast of Islay, but thankfully found a kindred spirit with the same degree of passion to develop the USA market of 340 million people. It is the expansion in this market above all others, especially in the early years, which has seen the Kilchoman brand develop so quickly.

With sales in the USA on an upward trajectory, Sam asked Anthony if he could supply them with single cask bottlings. Whilst this provided some headaches for the bottling team at Kilchoman, a regular supply of single casks started making their way to the USA, which eventually became the ImpEx Evolution series. Sam points out that very few distilleries produce small batch or single cask whiskies, because of the issues it creates within the bottling process. However, with a significant number of collectors in the USA, the single casks are extremely well received.

Import tariffs were an issue for the USA, with a 25% tariff being imposed by the Trump administration in 2019, which had a significant impact on the volume of whisky imported from Scotland. Anthony and Sam had a phone call where Anthony asked how he could help negate the impact of the tariffs. They agreed effectively to absorb half the costs each, so that there was no change in pricing, which ensured that they continued to do the same level of business. When ImpEx announced this, they received great feedback from both existing and new customers and Kilchoman certainly improved their standing in the US market.

Michael Fraser Milne is a Scotsman who has lived in New Zealand for many years. His relationship with Anthony is another which has stood the test of time.

He has been an importer of whisky to New Zealand since 1993 and started a retail shop, Whisky Galore in 2003. He travels to Scotland every year, and occasionally takes friends or customers round distilleries.

Michael remembers being with a small group who went over to Islay, early in 2006 and they arranged with Anthony to go and see him and the distillery. Kilchoman had just been established, but as yet was not producing whisky. Michael remembers it well because the day they arrived at the distillery, Kilchoman had just suffered from the kiln fire (12 February 2006).

As the small group approached the shop/office, Anthony came marching out and barged past them. Michael had no idea who Anthony was at this time, went into the office and upon indicating that they had an appointment to see Anthony he was advised that they had just missed him. They went back outside to see Anthony was clearly very flustered and said he didn't have time to meet with anyone that day as there was too much going on.

The group were eventually shown round by someone else and but for the bloody mindedness of Michael that might well have been that. However, unphased by the initial experience and still keen to develop a relationship with Kilchoman, he left his card and asked if Anthony, when he was less stressed, could give Michael a ring.

Anthony duly rang him and apologised for the issues on the day of the visit, Michael indicated that he was very keen to work with Kilchoman, when they had whisky to sell.

The following year, following an open invitation, Anthony and Kathy attended the Dramfest in Christchurch as guests of Michael and his wife Stella, and whilst he had no whisky at this stage, brought new make spirit and 12-month-old spirit over. Michael enjoyed the style of spirit that they were producing, he was impressed with the single-mindedness that Anthony was able to show in the face of all the doubters and so a relationship was established that endures to this day.

Michael recalls one unpleasant individual at the first Dramfest, who approached Anthony and asked to try his oldest whisky (bearing in mind he had new make and up to one year old spirit in February 2007). Anthony suggested that he go to some of the other stalls to try theirs, before coming back later. He did precisely that and came back later for his 'promised' aged dram and Anthony refused to serve him, saying that he was too drunk!

Michael accepts that the New Zealand market is one of the smaller markets for Kilchoman but feels that Anthony and Kathy have always gone out of their way as owners of the business to make them feel special. They have been over for every Dramfest (held every two years, where they have around 3,000 attendees) until the one last year, where they sent two brand ambassadors, and they always stay with each other in their respective homes.

Michael believes that Anthony has been generous to a fault with his time and knowledge in more recent years when assisting other distilleries.

There are many distilleries that have opened in the last 10 years or so, with stills of the same size and design as those at Kilchoman, trying to produce a similar type of new make spirit.

Michael also holds a great deal of respect for Kathy, whom he sees as the facilitator. Over much of the time they have known the Wills family, she was responsible for everything else at the distillery, which allowed Anthony to concentrate on producing the whisky. It is only in the last few years that she has taken some steps back to spend time with her growing family, but she still is able to exert influence over Anthony, so that decisions are not made in haste.

Since those early days, Whisky Galore has received every regular release from Kilchoman, throughout its 15 years of producing whisky, as well as a couple of single casks.

He recalls Peter Wills coming over to New Zealand to spend some time at a cricket academy, as part of his gap year. He was a passenger in a car accident with friends. The family contacted Michael and he and Stella gladly agreed to put Peter up for two or three weeks. Michael hadn't realised that Peter had been injured. There is a local cricket team in Greendale, and Michael sent him there to have a game. What he didn't realise was that Peter was still recovering from a piece of glass that had been removed from his rear in the accident and wasn't really fit to play, but didn't want to say anything given the hospitality he had been shown.

Whisky Galore distributes to over 1,000 businesses in New Zealand, many of them are very small, hotels, restaurants, off-licences, but there are some reasonably big retailers. They do local tours and tastings to promote the distilleries they work with. Kilchoman has a good loyal following in New Zealand.

Michael found out that Anthony wasn't a Keeper of the Quaich in 2018 (an honour bestowed upon individuals who have shown an outstanding commitment to the scotch whisky industry), so he wrote to the management committee. The normal procedure is that you submit a nomination, then get a seconder, but the Committee took it upon themselves to sponsor Anthony and made him a Keeper, effective immediately, a well-deserved honour.

In between bouts of working, they have socialised together, been to wineries, sailed on yachts, gone fly fishing, at which he says Kathy is particularly proficient and generally enjoyed each other's company.

All the world markets have a different back label relating to alcohol units, pregnancy warnings etc. The New Zealand one is no different and quite specific to their market. When they talk to some companies this is a real issue for them. When they speak to Kilchoman it is simply a question of "What do you want us to put on there?" – nothing is too much trouble.

Michael knows of no other distillery in Scotland where the founder and his family can complete all aspects of distilling, from starting up the stills, to bottling the whisky.

He recalls when Anthony and Kathy were last in New Zealand, he took them both out on a boat, but described Anthony as a 'nightmare', using nautical terms which Michael didn't understand, and generally behaving like Captain Pugwash. Not being regular sailors, Michael and Stella didn't have sailing jackets. When they went back to Kilchoman the following year, Anthony provided them with two Kilchoman sailing jackets, specially made for them, as a permanent reminder of good times and good friendship!

France has oft been quoted as the most important market for whisky exports outside of the USA. Anthony recognised this and was keen to set up distribution channels very early in the life of Kilchoman.

La Maison du Whisky (LMDW) was formed by Thierry Benitah's father Georges and his two brothers in 1956, opened its first shop in 1961 and another in 1968, then became an importer and distributor for whisky and other spirits, but mainly whisky. Thierry joined his father in the business in 1995 and grew the business. On his father's passing, Thierry took control of the business in the late 1990's. Today the business employs 240 people. There is lots of symmetry between the stories of Kilchoman and LMDW.

LMDW was able to take advantage of the new generation of distilleries that opened in the late 1990's/early 2000's, and Kilchoman was one of the key projects that LMDW became involved with.

Thierry knew Anthony before Kilchoman was set up, from his position as an independent bottler. There were relatively few people inhabiting this space at the time and most of them knew each other to some degree.

He was aware of the project when it was still in the discussion stage and followed the development with a very keen interest. Islay had always held a very special place in the whisky hierarchy for LMDW, mainly because the French consumers were lovers of Islay peated whisky. There was obviously going to be great interest in France in general, but in LMDW in particular, when a new distillery was being built on Islay.

In view of the importance of Islay to whisky drinkers in France, Thierry was travelling over to the island three or four times a year in the late 1990's. The establishment of a new distillery anywhere on Islay was not something that Thierry anticipated early in the 21st century and it went very much against the perceived wisdom at the time.

It was well in advance of the distillery being established that Anthony and Thierry had discussions about selling whisky (or spirit) in France. In the early 2000's in France there were not many companies distributing whisky. The larger players, such as Diageo and Pernod Ricard were there, but few smaller companies. LMDW were one of the only companies dealing with the independent distilleries.

France has about 5,000 independent retailers selling spirits and whisky is 80% of those sales. Servicing this market is complex, but LMDW over many years has proven an ability to access those retailers for the smaller independent distilleries that it works with.

For Thierry, having an Islay whisky in its portfolio was very significant, and the only other independent distillery on Islay at that time was Bruichladdich, which had just been resurrected by Mark Reynier and partners. Thierry considers that the development of the relationship with Kilchoman was one of the best strategic moves made by LMDW. It is an Islay whisky with a very transparent approach to how it produces whisky, something which his consumers embrace.

The intention was always for LMDW to be the distributor for the whole of France. To be responsible for growing the brand and leaving Anthony to concentrate more on other areas where he didn't have representation. That is not to say that Anthony didn't spend time in France, but he knew that Thierry would develop his brand. There was a trust evident from the earliest stage of the relationship, which still exists between the two businesses.

LMDW also has its own retail outlets and website (which was one of the first spirits websites in France), as well as the other 5,000 retail outlets in France, which helps to attract more people to the brand, but also provides general exposure of the brand.

The company started working with retailers in the 1980's. At that time, they were dealing with around 100 retailers. Now the number is around 3,500. There is a sales team of twenty working with these retailers, each taking an area with 100-150 retailers. They do masterclasses/tastings on the premises with promotional material, but more frequently, since COVID, they undertake online tastings.

Kilchoman is very supportive of their individual markets and will produce limited editions, small batches, single casks solely for France, and for LMDW. Overall, more than 1,500 customers buy Kilchoman from LMDW.

Thierry knew about Kilchoman in 2006 and earlier and tasted the new make spirit. The first order was a minimum of a pallet from Kilchoman in 2009. They were able to quickly ramp up sales as they had the network and were able to display in their shops, the only thing they didn't have was the whisky, which arrived in 2009.

It is difficult outside of France to understand the impact that a new Islay whisky had in France. Everyone was keen to try this 'nouveau du quartier' – this 'new kid on the block'. Thierry ensured that everyone in the whisky scene was aware of this sensational newcomer. There were other new launches of different products around this time, but only one Islay whisky. Thierry recalls Arran launching in 1995, but nothing else until Kilchoman in 2009 and this was an Islay whisky, the first new Islay in anyone's lifetime (discounting the relaunch of Bruichladdich).

Thierry had no doubt from day one that Kilchoman would be a success. It was exceptionally well received by the people of France. Nearly 1,000 customers buy the Machir Bay, although some only in very small quantities. Overall, between 1,500 and 2,000 customers buy some of the Kilchoman range every year in France. Without the support of LMDW, Kilchoman would not have anything like the same penetration in France.

Other Islay whiskies, which might be distributed by some of the major players, are represented in far fewer outlets. Part of the reason for the penetration is the fact that LMDW don't have the same marketing budget as some of the major players, so they had to ensure that their marketing produced results. The marketing was all done face to face with customers, using Anthony doing masterclasses and presentations, supported by Thierry and other members of the LMDW team.

Thierry and Anthony still speak whenever they need to and certainly on anything important. Their relationship remains strong. Most of the legwork is done by the two respective teams now, but the two principals still speak on a regular basis.

Brexit was expected to have some impact on the relationship between the two companies. It took many years for that to come to fruition. The first week of the transitional arrangements saw some upheaval, but frankly, apart from some delivery issues, which were down to customs, there was limited impact.

The first three months of the COVID pandemic were concerning, as no one knew what was going to happen longer term and companies were gearing up for a continuing impact over many more months and years. The reopening after the initial lockdown, saw a complete reversal of this.

However, during the last 12 months the reverse has been the case. During COVID, with so many people at home and furloughed from work, they spent more time online buying goods, with the money they weren't spending on travelling to work and holidays, and luxury goods such as malt whisky was one of the products being purchased. Also, customers were generally drinking more in the evenings, as they did not have to get up to go into work. Many people were also buying whisky for investment, as interest rates were so low.

The collapse in the market started in April 2023, when inflation rose quickly, there was overstocking at distributors, retailers and wholesalers, and disposable income was reducing, which meant that everyone was buying less whisky. It seems that the worst may now be past, and inventories have been reduced, people are gradually starting to buy whisky again, after 18 months, although many retailers are still discounting stock.

There are many distributors and importers who all undertake a fantastic job for Kilchoman and without whom they would have a difficult time penetrating foreign markets. Hopefully this chapter gives a flavour of the challenges faced by both Kilchoman and their distributors in a few of their key markets.

---◆◇◆---

Chapter 7

The Boys are Back in Town

It was never Anthony's intention, when establishing the distillery at Kilchoman, that he was creating a dynasty, or for this to be a place of employment for his children, or ultimately that the distillery would be run by one or all of them. It would be surprising however, if any parent didn't want their children to endorse what they had created, by becoming a part of it.

The family moved to Scotland in 1995 from Bristol, initially to the Kyles of Bute, and George recalls his father buying casks, then bottling them. The leftover casks were then fertile ground for teenagers who drained and tried what was left of the contents, screwing-up their faces at the taste – they would not embrace whisky for some years yet. The barrels were then cut up into planters.

At the time Kathy's father was living at Laggan on Islay and she wanted to be closer to him. Both Anthony and Kathy were happy to move to Scotland, but probably for their separate reasons. The boys just were happy so long as they were playing sports. They spent three weeks of the summer holidays every year at Laggan with their grandad.

All the boys played a lot of sport at school and Anthony rarely missed a sports match, so had to juggle his life as an independent bottler with the sporting aspirations of his children.

George is the eldest of the three, being born in 1985. The other two were conveniently spaced out at two-year intervals, James in 1987 and Peter in 1989. All three boys attended Glenalmond School in Perthshire, (founded by William Gladstone in 1847) on a boarding basis, from the age of thirteen and Peter would have been around fifteen when his father first advised them of the move to Islay.

The first recollection that the boys have of a conversation about creating a distillery was late 2001, which coincidentally was the same time as the Kilchoman Distillery Company was incorporated (12 November 2001).

There was no discussion with the boys at this time, it was just snippets of information they picked up on.

It was probably not until around March 2004, after the initial round of fundraising, when building work was just commencing on the distillery that they found out that they were moving to their grandparents' house at Laggan on Islay, and they moved over later in the year. James recalls his dad sitting the three boys down at the dinner table to tell them, although Peter's recollection was that they were travelling at the time they were told.

The move was in 2004, George had started a terminal year at Northumbria University, James was studying for A Levels and Peter approaching his GCSE's. None of them had any idea what lay ahead and how their own lives would become inextricably linked with the distillery ambitions of their father.

Peter can recall the stills being moved in, which was in 2005. After that most of the holidays, for all three of them, either from school or from university, were spent initially painting rafters and skirtings in the café/visitor area and following the opening they could be found in the café serving teas, coffees and cakes. Thankfully they were able to develop skills in sales and marketing, because they certainly wouldn't have made any money waiting on – they can all recall spilling something over their paying guests.

As time and skills progressed Peter and James especially remember taking tours, and working in the maltings, mainly doing labouring jobs and earning a little pocket money.

None of the boys were interested in whisky at the time the distillery was built and even though they were surrounded by maturing casks, for all of them there was no epiphanal moment, when whisky 'found' them. When Peter was 17 or 18, he did more of the production work at the distillery and became more interested in whisky, but still didn't like it as a drink of choice.

In the summer of 2005 James left college and the distillery was still not open. James assisted at the distillery, prepping it for opening, but went travelling to Australia for six months, from early 2006. On his return he would help in the café, filled a few casks, and did a lot of sweeping up!

James went to Newcastle University and Peter and George (briefly) went to Northumbria. James studied marketing and business. He was uncertain in his choice of eventual career, but he is probably the most creative of the three siblings (by their admission and his) and marketing was a natural choice, so he thought.

George is first to admit that he was far from a model pupil when it came to the discipline of learning. There was never any likelihood of him going to Oxford, Cambridge or Edinburgh University. He went briefly to Northumbria University to study land management, but after a year, found that university was not for him, so started working in hospitality, where he remained for about nine or ten years.

Initially working on the West coast of Scotland, George then moved down to the Chester/Wrexham area and ran some country pubs there. That suited him in that he learnt the business, grew to understand customers and what they were looking for and generally it provided an excellent apprenticeship to the business he ended up being a part of.

James' dissertation in his third year at university was on 'Factors affecting the consumer's choice of single malt', a literary masterpiece that will unfortunately never see the light of day, unless one of his tutors has retained a copy (please DM me if you have a copy)! James freely admits that his original effort was terrible and if he wrote such an article now it would be hugely different. Someone must have taken pity on him as he ultimately received a 2:1, by less than 1%. He suggests that if that had been a 2:2 he would have joined the army and Kilchoman may never have employed him. Such are life's serendipitous moments.

After his gap year, James worked for Funkin, a company in London that made fruit purees and pre-mixed cocktails. He was in London for three or four years, working that market. He had lots of friends and acquaintances working in London, so it was a natural fit for the lifestyle he wanted at that time.

After nearly four years of working in London, James professed to being a little bored, so he approached his dad and asked if he had anything available for him. It was probably not a lengthy conversation in 2013, and James started at Kilchoman at a time when all the funding issues had passed, Machir Bay had been launched and Kilchoman was on the up and up. He has however, subsequently played a major role in the development of the business.

Peter did a generic marketing degree at Northumbria University. Whilst at university he grew to understand more about whisky and production and had represented the Kilchoman brand at a few of the whisky shows across the UK.

At no stage was he ever pushed into working for Kilchoman by his dad. When he had finished university, he spoke with Anthony suggesting that he would like to work in the industry for Kilchoman. His dad pointed him in the direction of London, where he saw potential for appreciable development, and there were some key 'off trade' accounts, which Anthony was struggling to service and effectively Peter was left to get on with it.

He left university in June and went down to London. It was not a full-time role at this stage. Peter wanted to enjoy his life in London, something which all three boys have in common, and work was probably an adjunct to his personal enjoyment at that stage. Kilchoman had started releasing whisky the previous year, so Anthony needed someone in London to sell it.

Whilst he was trying to get his feet under whatever table was available, he met, or was introduced to, a lot of people in the industry. Colin Dunn of Diageo was one who assisted a young pretender and competitor at an early stage of his development. Colin was known to Anthony, had been up to Islay regularly and had been a vocal supporter of the distillery from its inception. Colin passed on tips as to how to approach selling the brand and introduced Peter to more influential people in the industry. Anyone who knows Colin will inevitably have benefitted at some stage from his sage advice on everything from whisky to the drinking dens of St Ives.

The early days in 2010 and 2011 were very tough. Peter had young whisky, he was a young presenter, who by his own admission looked 18, trying to sell to a group of middle-aged men, who all liked to drink 20-year-old Speyside whisky. Peter was inexperienced, he knew all about Kilchoman, but his knowledge of the wider whisky industry was limited at that time. His days and evenings consisted of lots of cold calling, knocking on unreceptive doors.

Anthony was very much of the 'sink or swim' mentality. Prior to one of his first tastings in front of 40 or 50 people where he had to talk for 90 minutes, Peter asked his dad for advice. Anthony provided him with a couple of paragraphs and a "just talk about whisky" reply – not ideal for a 21-year-old, looking 18, with limited wider knowledge, but it did allow Peter to develop his own style of presenting.

James joined the business as well during this time, so their roles developed together, as joint ambassadors for the business. It was much easier to travel out of London than it was from Islay, so it made sense to be based there. Peter lived on James' sofa for about a year when they were both in London.

Peter was looking after the London 'on-trade', Asia, when they started travelling more, as well as half of Europe. When James joined, he took on the remainder of Europe and North and South America. James was slanted more towards marketing and design and Peter towards sales. Peter enjoyed the travelling and engaging with people around the world in those early years.

For George, with his life away from the family running pubs in Cheshire, the work was excellent from the point of view of a grounding in the 'on trade' side of the business. The only drawback was that this was all-consuming, with little social life outside of the pub, so on one of his returns to Islay, he had a discussion with his dad, who said that Kilchoman was looking for someone to help with sales within the UK. By that time James and Peter were already working for the business and George wasn't sure whether it was the right move for him.

George made the decision to join the family business in April 2014, a move which he was initially uncertain about, but which, over time, has proved to have been an unqualified success.

In 2014, his role was in UK sales and marketing. Originally, that involved working with Gordon McPhail, who were the UK distributors at that time. Initially he had to find out where Kilchoman was being sold within the UK. James and Peter were spending a lot of time travelling abroad and working out of London, so the UK had almost been neglected. He recalls his first job was putting a map together of the places that Kilchoman was being sold in the UK and finding out where it wasn't.

There was obviously some overlap between the boys at this stage, each had their key markets, James in France and the USA, George in the UK and Peter in Germany and the Far East/Australasia. However, they all did some travelling to other market sectors such as eastern Europe in the early days, to assist in the development of those areas.

George believes that Gordon McPhail was a perfect fit for Kilchoman during the early years, from 2010 onwards, because of their network, which meant Kilchoman was placed into many retail outlets. However, as time went on, Gordon McPhail concentrated on their own brands, which meant that Kilchoman, although it was sold, did not have anyone directly marketing and selling their whiskies.

In 2014, Anthony decided to change their UK distributor to Pol Roger, known more for their distribution of champagne and wine, but known to Anthony from his previous life as a wine distributor. They are also involved with Glenfarclas, with whom Kilchoman has traditionally had close contact. Pol Roger wanted another whisky brand with family links in their portfolio, Kilchoman would be very much at the forefront of their marketing, so it seemed a good fit. Pol Roger was also very well connected with higher end hotels and restaurants, something Kilchoman was keen to exploit.

The role of all three siblings was and to a certain extent still is, talking to distributors, ensuring that they have all the information they need, putting together any adverts that budgets allowed them to make. Back in 2012/2013, everything was discussed with Anthony, who was copied in on every email. Gradually over the following 10-year period, much more control has been ceded to the boys and their team. They provided quarterly reports on their regions and if they were on Islay they would have discussions on a multitude of other things or do so by conference call if away (which is most of the time).

Peter was in London for around nine years. The nature of his work evolved from the first two or three years, which was almost purely focussed on London. At that early stage, until 2012/3 exports were very limited, but that started to change. Part of his remit in the early days was the development of a website, beyond the two pages that existed for several years. Very few distilleries at this time were using social media in any form at all, and Peter, with the sales team started to use social media as a sales tool.

It was probably around 2012/3 when Kilchoman was 6/7 years old that Peter started to see a change in the perception of Kilchoman, which manifested itself in significant increases in sales in Europe. Germany suddenly started ordering multiple pallets of whisky rather than a few cases a couple of times a month (Seventy cases of six bottles to the pallet in the EU). The knock-on effect of this was that there was a need to upgrade the bottling line, review whether they were producing enough, and ensuring that they had core range products, sufficient to supply this increased demand.

From James' perspective there was some marked change in the importance of Kilchoman to the distributors in his regions, but he saw this as being something which was on a slower trajectory than Peter had seen in Germany and happened a little later. Around 2016 he noticed that distributors were contacting them, rather than the other way round, and rather than being a hard sell, many distributors were asking them for more of their whisky.

The development has been assisted by the marketing team at Kilchoman being allocated a greater budget, which again opens more channels with the distributors. It is traditional within the industry that distributors are given a percentage of the whisky they purchase as a budget for promoting. In the early days of Kilchoman, Anthony was not able to offer that, but as time progressed, this became part of the marketing budget, but not until around 2017/8. My earliest recollection of going to Fèis, was that there was never a free dram of anything. Thankfully Anthony has loosened the purse strings a little in recent years, so there is an occasional dram awaiting!

James is based in Edinburgh along with Peter, they both moved up there in 2019, when Kilchoman opened an office. Also, there is Ken Langenfeld, a French/Spanish speaking Scot, which is handy, especially as France is now one of the biggest markets for Kilchoman and Emma McHarrie, both of whom joined the sales team in the last couple of years. It provides a hub where travel to the continent and further afield is much easier, but they can easily travel over to Islay should that prove necessary.

Throughout the period from 2010, when Peter started in the business, through 2012, when James joined and 2014, when George started, the boys have prepared marketing reports for their respective regions and presented these at board meetings. Their involvement at board meetings, usually on a quarterly basis, was the extent of their report. They did not get involved in the wider decision-making process, any discussions regarding expansion and development took place between Anthony and Niels.

Over time that has changed, with the boys sitting in on full board meetings and providing input on all matters concerning the distillery. Now they are all involved in discussions about capital expenditure, cashflow, expansion plans and strategy, as well as their traditional marketing and sales input.

It has been a natural progression where the boys have taken over more of the marketing and sales side of the business. All the distillery-based operations, production and new buildings, remain in the overall control of Anthony and he still retains full control of the blending and vatting of releases.

It was in 2019 that Kilchoman decided to take over their own distribution in the UK. It was felt that they now had sufficient knowledge of their home market and the team to support this. The two distributors had taken their product as far as they were able, but Anthony and the boys felt that by taking the distribution in house and combining that with stronger marketing, they would have a greater reach.

George's role changed massively at this stage as it was his responsibility to ensure greater market penetration, that their products were marketed to the full extent, and that sales figures continued in their upward trend.

James looks after the French market, although Ken, who is a French speaker, travels over there on a regular basis. Clearly James recognises the benefits of long-term relationships, which allows much more frank discussions on such issues as pricing and margins. Many of Kilchoman's relationships are very long standing and all the boys recognise the worth of these relationships.

There is a tendency to outgrow some of the distributors, as was shown with Gordon Macphail and Pol Roger in the UK, although this is usually due to the size of the distributor, where Kilchoman now need companies with a significant reach in their markets. Andy Dunn, in Alberta, Canada was one such example, who was effectively a 'one man band' and had done great work in the early days promoting the business in Canada. Kilchoman needed to go beyond just the specialist shops which he was used to dealing with, so were forced to change distributors for greater penetration.

ImpEx Beverages in the USA and La Maison du Whisky in France are both sizeable businesses and fit with Kilchoman's ethos of wanting to do business with people, but alongside that, having a significant presence in their own market. These distributors can look five years into the future and be part of the planning process alongside Kilchoman.

Pricing is so important to George as the last thing he wants to hear from retailers is that they can't order any more of a particular line because it is still stuck on the shelf gathering dust. Since it was launched in 2012, the price of Machir Bay has risen by less than £10, which considering the way in which some distilleries have been raising prices on all their whiskies, represents a very positive declaration of intent by Kilchoman.

To ensure maximum penetration within the UK market, Kilchoman is continually looking to recruit staff within the UK, to ensure constant contact with customers, and increased exposure through tastings.

George feels that Kilchoman has been very fortunate with the team that have come to work for them. Their enthusiasm and product knowledge shines through. As the recruitment for these roles is undertaken by the boys, they want to work with similar minded individuals, who have that same level of enthusiasm and desire to succeed. That indeed is evident across all the Kilchoman team from the serving staff in the restaurant, to the visitor centre, to the production team. Everyone is an ambassador and salesperson for the distillery. The intention seems to be that all Kilchoman staff will carry that Kilchoman DNA.

Overall, the Kilchoman team numbers forty-seven, which for a modern distillery is high, but it evidences Anthony's belief that people make whisky, and people also sell that whisky. The business would rather recruit, where it can, from Islay, but that is proving extremely difficult, simply because there aren't the numbers of available personnel. Adding the fact that the sales and marketing jobs involve a lot of travel round the UK and abroad, living on Islay seems to be a disadvantage in that arena.

Catherine Macmillan manages the social media, which is a growing part of the Kilchoman operation. She works with individuals and companies to put together content. Kilchoman has for the last few years spent money on social media campaigns, recognising the importance of social media amongst the younger generation, who ultimately will be the drivers of any significant growth.

Coming up with innovative ideas is not solely down to the sales and marketing management team, they welcome the views of any member of the team and many of the current initiatives are the result of collaboration. They are conscious that social media does not have to be cinema graphic content, it can be much simpler and often it is the simplicity of ideas, which creates better content.

All the distillery team are very used to having a camera thrust into their face and asked to talk through what they are doing. Such content on the website and social media leads to a better understanding of processes, but in a simple hands-on way. It also introduces a wider public to many members of the Kilchoman production team.

The biggest asset Kilchoman has is their team and it is the flexibility of the team and the ability to respond quickly to situations if they need to, which creates a differentiator from many other distilleries.

The marketing team are constantly feeding back market expectations and desires. Openness and integrity are at the heart of everything that they do in terms of marketing, and they genuinely listen to feedback from customers and distributors alike. That is one of the reasons why 2024 saw the introduction of a Sanaig Cask Strength, because customers have been requesting it for a number of years and the time and stocks of mature Oloroso casks was right.

The European, USA tours were introduced in 2014 and have been a resounding success, so much so that the marketing team added a Far East tour in 2024. In 2023 they estimate they have met around 5,000 individuals on the European tour, many of whom had never previously heard of or tried Kilchoman.

Kilchoman's marketing team are constantly reviewing what they are putting out into the market and comparing that to what others are doing. There is a significant difference between Kilchoman's output and most other distilleries.

Production of single casks is something that allows Kilchoman to stand out from other distilleries. With Anthony's background in releasing single casks, it made perfect sense to him to do that at Kilchoman, despite the protestations of the bottling team! Other distilleries do not have the bottling capabilities on site and must book in times for bottling, which is where the Kilchoman's flexibility is key. They do have to ship bottles and labels onto Islay and then the bottles back off, but they are able to control what and when they bottle.

The labelling is becoming a challenge, as every country has brought in laws relating to their own bottles. There used to be one label for UK, one for general export and one for the USA. Over the years that has changed. Italy, France, Australia and others need a recycling label, specific to their country. The bottling manager Derek Scott has a particular mistrust of the marketing team, whenever they do a collaborative or private vatting, or any bottling for export.

Kathy and Anthony are incredibly proud of the contribution their sons have made to the business over the years they have been involved. They have every reason to suspect that the business is in good hands moving forward.

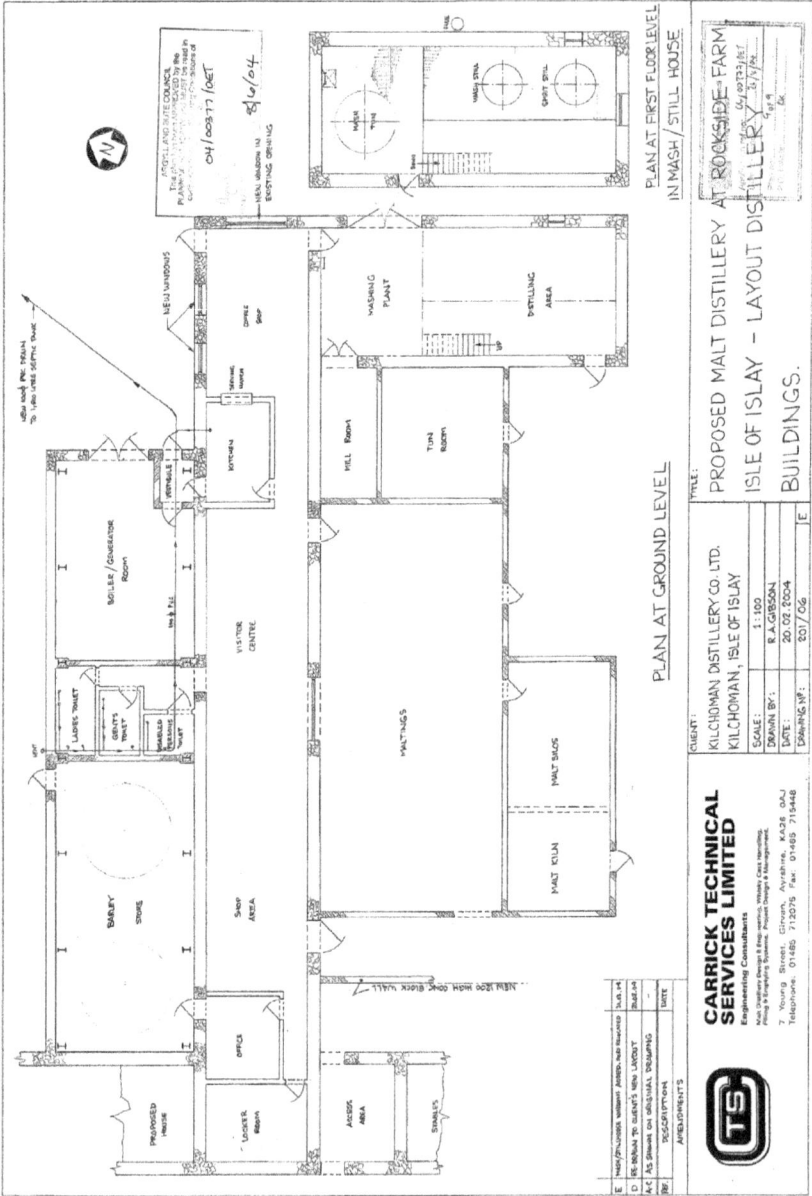

Carrick Technical Services Ltd Original plans for the Distillery 2004

Door of the old cattle shed signed by all visitors to the Feis event 31/05/2004

Still house before work commenced early 2005

Anthony and Kathy painting still house – Pre health and safety!

Visitor Centre in 2004 before work started

Visitor Centre 2005 after works completed

Original Mill buildings that became the Still House and Visitor Centre

Still House and Visitor Centre under construction 2005

Pagoda on the Still House under construction 2005

Arrival of the Stills and Mash Tun

2005 Bonded Warehouse Steels in place

Inside the Bonded Warehouse

First Cask Filled December 14th 2005

First casks laid down in the Warehouse 2006

After the Kiln Fire 2006

The Rebuilt Kiln Building 2006

The Kiln after rebuilding 2006

2008 In Anticipation Bottlings

Anthony and Kathy at the Launch of the Inaugural release

Anthony and Niels Ladefoged with the First Bottle from the First Cask

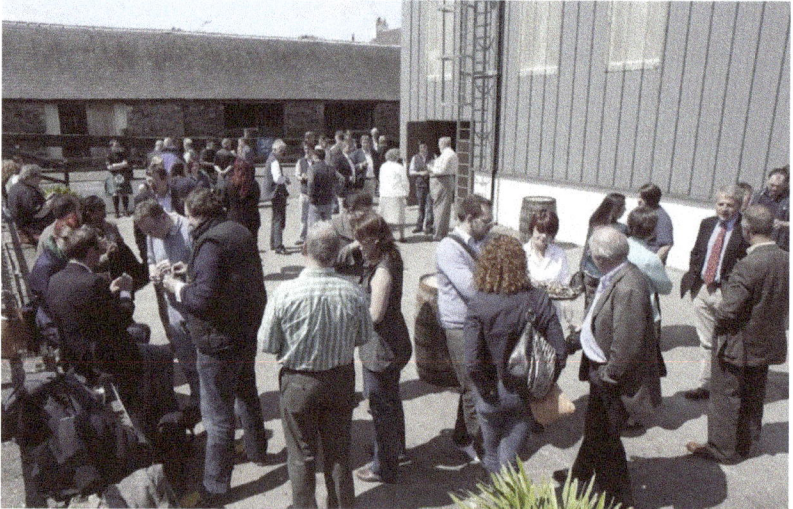

2011 Launch of Kilchoman's 100% Islay

Kilchoman winners of the 2012 Islay Beach Rugby Tournament

Start of Construction of Warehouses at Coninsby

Aerial Photo of the Warehouse Works at Conisby

2014 Improvements in the Bottling Hall

2014 Installation of New Vatting Tanks

George with the Liveried Landrover ready to go on tour in 2015

Aerial View of Kilchoman in 2015

Celebration of Kilchoman's 10 Year Anniversary in 2015

Jim Swan - A major influence on the Distillery Spirit for over 10 years

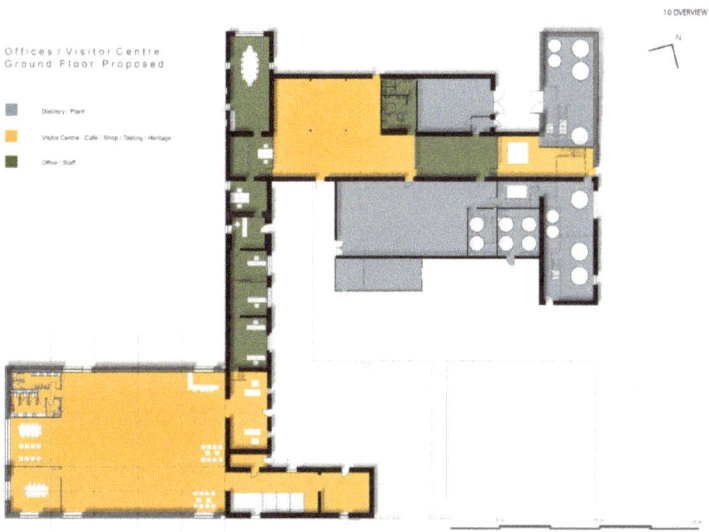

2017 Development Plans by AHR Architects

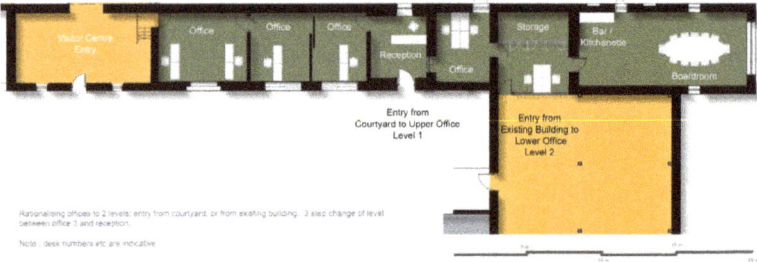

2017 Office Conversion per AHR Architects

2017 Visitor Centre Development AHR Architects

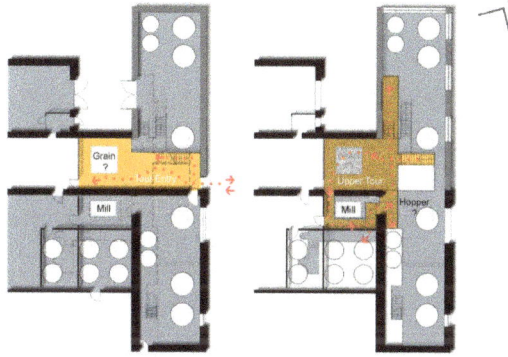

2017 Still Extension AHR Architects

2018 New Warehousing – Robinsons

2019 Kiln and Malt Store

2019 Upgraded Still House

2019 Inside the Still House

2019 Visitor Centre from Rear

2020 Opening of the Visitor Centre

Kilchoman Barley Fields surrounding the Distillery

2021 Kilchoman Distillery from the Rear

Site of the Proposed Rum Distillery in Barbados

Fun At Feis

Anthony with Duffy MacNeil 2012

The Visitor Centre 2012

In the courtyard 2016

2018 Hoopla

Islay Heads peat cutting 2018

James Wills with the liveried Landrover

Peter Wills Prior to a masterclass 2018

The Wills boys entertaining the crowd

2018 Another Anthony Masterclass

James, Anthony and Peter 2022

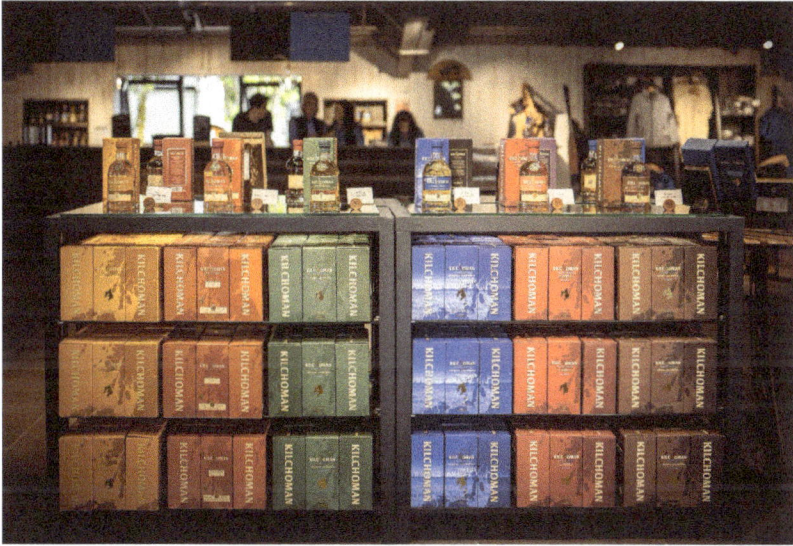

2023 Feis colours of Kilchoman

2023 Feis Drone shot

2023 Feis in the Courtyard

2023 Islay Pipe Band

The lull before the storm - Feis 2023

All Quiet at present - Feis 2023

Chapter 8

Per ardua ad astra

As the company moved into a state of profitability and Anthony could spend more time at the distillery planning, in 2012/3 they were filling about 21 casks per week, mostly fresh ex-bourbon barrels from Buffalo Trace, as well as some sherry butts. His intention was to significantly increase production over the coming years and had to plan how that could be done.

In April 2013, a heat exchanger was installed at the wash still. The wash still was previously charged with 3,000 litres of fresh wash at a temperature of 20C, and after the first distillation, 2,000 litres of hot effluent (pot ale) at a temperature of about 99C was discharged. With the new heat exchanger, the heat from the effluent was now transferred to the fresh wash, preheating it to around 70C. This shortened the boiling time from 55 to 25 minutes, which resulted in a significant saving of steam energy.

Loch Gorm was also released in April 2013. Named after the dark peaty loch near to the distillery, Kilchoman decided to follow the naming tradition that had been established with Machir Bay, which now gives the previous year's uninspiringly named Sherry Cask a more evocative name. The whisky won a gold medal at the IWSC Awards (International Wine and Spirits Competition) later in the year. For a distillery trying to establish its reputation in the market, such awards are gratefully received, although more established distilleries and prominent whisky writers tend to offer considerably less enthusiasm, unless of course the writers happen to find themselves on a judging panel.

September 2013 saw the completion of the 10,000 cask warehousing at Conisby. Dunnage warehousing for casks is the Kilchoman preferred (but considerably less practical) way, with casks up to three high in the warehouse, which ensures a reasonably even maturation across the various cask types. Casks are simply left in place until they are required for bottling.

Modern warehousing which can see casks stacked up to nine or ten high, leads to uneven maturation, with those higher casks maturing more quickly, so if there is not a system of cask rotation, or regular sampling, this can create issues with the whisky. More and more companies are using racking, which makes removal of the casks so much easier and enables stacking of casks up to eight or nine high.

Unlike traditional Dunnage warehouses, the decision was made to concrete the entire floor and not just the paths between the rows of casks. These additional warehouses allowed Kilchoman to retrieve all their casks scattered across the island.

At the end of the 2013, Kilchoman reported production of 130,000 litres of pure alcohol.

In January 2014, two vatting tanks were installed in Warehouse No.1, to be used to marry a large volume of casks, for significant bottlings such as Machir Bay and 100% Islay. Prior to this the company had relied on Bruichladdich for assistance, the casks were taken to Bruichladdich, married and then returned to the Kilchoman bottling hall in IBC's.

At this time, improvements were also made to the malt transport system from the malting floor to the kiln. The bottling hall was equipped with a new machine for applying corks to the bottles and new conveyor belts. A far cry from the days of filling bottles from teapots!

One of the significant markets that Kilchoman had not yet touched was the travel retail market and in March 2014, they dipped a toe into this area (over the next few years travel retail lost its importance as most bottles became available online and the airport exclusives generally became a thing of the past). Their first travel retail exclusive bottling was Coull Point (bottles had been available since the end of 2013 in some areas). Following its chosen path of naming releases after West Coast Islay landmarks, Coull Point is a rugged headland just north of Machir Bay.

The business had been purchasing different casks for a few years now, to see how the spirit reacted with wines and fortified wines. In August 2014, they bottled the first of these more exotic casks, which was a Port Cask Release, a full maturation in Ruby Port casks, which were filled in 2011. This was the next stage in the Kilchoman evolution, proof positive that the Kilchoman spirit worked exceptionally well with a wide range of casks, as the next ten years would prove beyond any doubt.

The previous year and playing on their connection with Land Rover, the marketing team undertook a tour of the UK, in a Kilchoman badged Land Rover, selling the Kilchoman brand and whisky. Following on from this, in September 2014, Peter and James Wills, embarked on a marketing tour with the Kilchoman Land Rover that took them to distributors in eight European countries; Belgium, Luxembourg, Holland, Germany, Austria, Italy, Switzerland and France. This was extremely well received, and the tours have continued in Europe and the USA since then, with an interruption during the COVID outbreak.

During 2014, for the first time Kilchoman filled more than 1,000 casks, which they saw as necessary due to the upward trajectory of sales. They estimated that 150,000 bottles were sold. To ensure that the lines of sales and production didn't get too close, they needed to increase production. With the wonderful rose-tinted glasses of hindsight, Anthony wishes that they had produced a lot more spirit in the early days. That, however, would have put a great deal more stress on a workforce and management team, who were already putting in long hours, and in the early days there was no visible return.

Whisky was rapidly becoming a commodity, not just a drink and the next seven or eight years were to prove a time of massive development for Kilchoman. The start of this development was the purchase of Rockside Farm in 2015. Mark French had been very supportive in the early years of the distillery and the agreement worked well for both parties, in that Mark was paid a premium price for the barley he produced, and Anthony had the location, the initial set up and now a distillery producing 150,000 bottles a year.

It had been the initial plan to build a farm distillery and Kilchoman was already that and more. With all three of the boys on board there was a need as Anthony saw it, to create something more than a small farm distillery. Mark didn't want anything more than a small distillery and visitor numbers and operations at the distillery were appreciably more than he had anticipated. This created some conflict and with the board having plans to expand further, which Mark was completely against, they were at something of an impasse.

The solution was for Kilchoman to buy Rockside Farm, which was completed in June 2015, with the French family leaving the farm in November. Despite their differences at the end of the agreement, Anthony looks back with gratitude that Mark was instrumental in getting the project off the ground, at the place ultimately that was the perfect location. Who knows, but for Rockside farm being where it is, had the distillery been built near to the Wills' house, might have been called Laggan, which somehow doesn't have the same cachet as Kilchoman.

This now meant that Kilchoman had full control over the whole process of 'barley to bottle' but would also have to commit to running the farm.

In April 2015 Kilchoman launched Sanaig, named after a rocky inlet near the distillery, and was initially only distributed in Belgium, Germany, France and the Netherlands. Like Machir Bay, it is a vatting of sherry and bourbon casks and bottled in batches with no age statement. Sanaig has a much higher sherry cask content than Machir Bay and was so well received that at the start of 2016 Kilchoman made Sanaig its second general release.

During 2015 John MacLellan, the Distillery Manager was living with prostate cancer. Kilchoman wanted to do something to support the Beatson Cancer Charity, which was helping John, so they auctioned off the first bottle of a 10-year-old whisky at auction. The bottle contained whisky drawn from the first cask laid down on 14 December 2005, and was hand bottled by Anthony on 14 December 2015 – precisely 10 years after its distillation. The auction, which ran from 7–14 December, was open to bidders around the world through the distillery's website. The bottle raised £7,000 and that amount was rounded up to £10,000 by the Distillery. John passed away on March 27, 2016, a massive loss to the distillery and his family.

When John McLellan died in 2016, there was clearly a need to replace him, and Anthony was keen to promote internally if there was an appropriate candidate, and there was, in the form of Robin Bignal, who started working for Kilchoman in 2010 on a part-time basis. He had no background in whisky and at that time, he was a self-employed farmer, working on his parents' farm and others around Islay and did a bit of geese control on the island. It was John MacLellan who mentioned to Robin that there was part time work available at the distillery. His original role was as a stillman/mashman.

Robin became involved with tasting and nosing, which Anthony took the lead role in, but Robin had been doing it for six years and was very good at knowing when a cask was ready to be bottled. Robin now looks after the production side.

To complement the purchase of the farm, Kilchoman needed to appoint a General Manager to oversee the running of the farm and the whole of the barley to bottle concept, which was at the very heart of the Kilchoman philosophy. Distillery Manager roles vary considerably from place to place. Here the role was effectively split in 2016 with Islay Heads being appointed as General Manager to oversee all aspects of the distillery and the farm and Robin as Production Manager to oversee the production process.

Islay came with a track record in estate management, having been Assistant Estate Manager at the Dunlossit Estate on Islay and is a true Ileach, fully embracing and overseeing every part of the unique barley to bottle whisky-making process. You are just as likely to see Islay at the wheel of a tractor or combine harvester, as chatting to guests in the visitor centre or liaising with outside contractors, such is the variety of his role.

Some Distillery/Production Managers are very eloquent and sell the business far and wide, others like to get their hands dirty in the day-to-day grind of distillery operations – that is Robin. He is an engineer, who would much rather have his hands full with an oily rag, than a script to read to waiting officianados. John MacLellan was a great raconteur, as are other Islay favourites like Jim McEwan, but Robin quietly and efficiently gets on with the job of producing whisky.

During September and October 2016, Kilchoman's marketing team undertook the USA East Coast Tour. This was the first time they had travelled to the USA. James and Peter Wills, in the liveried Land Rover travelled from Boston through the US states of Connecticut, Rhode Island, New York, New Jersey, Delaware, Pennsylvania, Maryland and all the way to Washington DC, conducting numerous tastings to critical acclaim (the whisky and their presenting skills) along the way.

On 14 February 2017, the death of Dr Jim Swan was announced. Jim had been massively influential during the setting up of the distillery and Anthony gave this tribute:

"Everyone at Kilchoman is immensely sad to hear of Jim's death. One of the best bits of advice I had when setting up the distillery was to get Jim involved. I knew the style of whisky I wanted to produce and thought I knew the problems I was going to face but I'm not sure I would have succeeded without Jim's wealth of knowledge. He designed our stills, was always available to assure me that I was doing a good job and giving me the confidence I needed in those early days. He

was here during the first spirit runs and on trying the spirit, he smiled and said 'if you look after this you could bottle it after 3 years' and we haven't looked back since.

Jim's continued support has played a massive part in Kilchoman's success and I will always be very grateful for his contribution. Quiet, unassuming and irreplaceable, he became a dear friend to the Kilchoman family."

There is nothing more to be said, many distilleries owe a great deal to Jim Swan.

In April 2018, the new kiln and malt floor building, started in 2017, was completed, which doubled the capacity for malting their own barley. The reason for the expansion was simply so they could produce more 100% Islay. Anthony had been concerned that as the output of the distillery increased, the amount of their 100% Islay reduced as an overall proportion of what they produced, so he wanted to produce more of it. The intention going forward is to make whisky using 30% of their own barley, but this was becoming increasingly difficult with expansion of the distillery and the lack of acreage immediately available to plant barley.

The new malting floor allowed up to four tonnes of barley to be malted per week. This new building also gave the distillery the flexibility to vary the phenol content of the 100% Islay malt (which was previously around 20 ppm) in the future, although there was no specific plan to do so.

The new kiln and malting floor were just the first of a series of construction measures planned over the next two years, intended to double production capacity. The still house would be extended and equipped with two new stills of identical shape and size to the existing stills to ensure a consistency of product, and a second mash tun was to be fitted. The number of washbacks would also be increased from 6 to 14.

Over time, several new warehouses were planned to accommodate the significantly increased amount of newly filled casks, and a new, much larger visitor centre was planned by converting and extending the former pony stables.

At this stage the marketing team was in full flow and a further innovation in November 2018 saw the introduction of NFC Labels. Kilchoman was one of the first Scottish whisky distilleries to introduce Near Field Communication (NFC) labels on its two general releases Machir Bay and Sanaig. By means of NFC and tapping their smart phone against the label, buyers can obtain further information about the bottlings, such as tasting notes, details of the casks used and other information about limited releases from Kilchoman.

In May 2019, Kilchoman released their first STR Cask Matured whisky. Shaving, toasting and re-charring of casks was the brainchild of Jim Swan, and this release was a homage to Jim.

To achieve an STR cask, the inner surface of used red wine casks is first shaved to reveal a surface of fresh oak with relatively low red wine saturation. The inner surface is then toasted, over an oak chip fire made from used cask staves. This leads to a caramelisation of the sugars and vanillins contained in the fresh wood. Finally, the cask is burnt out (re-charred) to ensure a high level of flavour extraction from the wood. Overall, this unsurprisingly leads to a much more subtle red wine note within the whisky stored in this cask than is the case with unprocessed red wine casks.

By August 2019, the next phase of the building works was completed. The stillhouse extension, including the installation of a panoramic window in the gable of the new stillhouse, which doubled its original length and includes two new stills identical in size and shape, a new mash-tun and a new malt transport system. Six new washbacks were installed in the rear part of the old malting floor. This increased the distillery's maximum production to 640,000 litres of alcohol per year.

This programme of expansion works was started in 2017 with the construction of the new kiln/malting floor building, completed in 2018. Extension of the stillhouse and the installation of the new equipment was completed in 2019 and at that time it was anticipated that the new visitor centre would be completed by early 2020. Alongside this work, further warehouses were being built to accommodate the increase in filled casks. In 2018, Kilchoman was filling 38 casks per week and this number was expected to rise to over 100 casks per week and beyond by 2022, so significantly more storage space would be required.

Kathy believes the expansion of the business in 2018/9 would not have happened if the boys had not come into the business. They would have kept the business as a farm distillery, as was the original intended ethos. Anthony wanted a legacy to continue for the boys and therefore put forward the bold expansion plans to double the output, which effectively meant redesigning the whole operation and introducing the new visitor centre.

The visitor centre was designed by Kathy's sister, Nicola Wilks, who had designed the original shop and café areas. This time she had a much broader palate on which to paint.

They wanted to keep the farm feel, with entry from the car park, through the farmyard and stables. They wanted to build a modern, open, airy building where people could relax in armchairs and have a dram, browse through merchandise, both Kilchoman and from other suppliers and eat and drink in the café. The atmosphere here is now enhanced by the attitude of the staff, who all appear to enjoy working in that space for Kilchoman. At the height of the season, there are now around fourteen staff employed in the visitor centre. The business has come a long way, from its very humble beginnings nearly twenty years ago, when Kathy did a great deal of the work in the café/visitor centre.

The overall costs of the expansion programme were in the region of £6 million, which was unheard of ten years earlier, but which the banks were more than willing to fund, given the extent of their stocks and current and projected sales volumes. Although Kilchoman was still a long way behind its more elderly neighbours on Islay, in terms of litres of alcohol produced per annum, this current expansion programme and subsequent plans, was a significant step towards those other distilleries.

In September 2019 extension work on the malt store was completed. The old kiln building would continue to be used as a malt warehouse, and this building was extended to improve capacity.

⸺◈⸺

Chapter 9

The COVID years and beyond

2020 started well, and on Friday 21 February, Kilchoman invited around 150 guests comprising family, friends, colleagues and business partners to the opening of the new still house and visitor centre. This marked the completion of the £6 million expansion programme started in 2017, which aimed to double production capacity to meet the increasing demand for Kilchoman around the world.

The last phase of the expansion programme, and the one closest to the heart of Kathy Wills, was the completion of a new visitor centre with shop and café. Kathy had wanted to ensure that the visitor centre was spacious and homely, to enable guests to spend time soaking in the atmosphere, having a dram, whilst enjoying some of the excellent food/coffee/cakes that Kilchoman had become renowned for. I have seen people devour four mugs of Cullen Skink on Fèis day, such was its appeal! One of the former pony stables was converted into the café and a large extension with a shop area, tasting rooms with picture windows, comfortable armchair seating, a fire for the winter and a bar was built.

This final piece of the Kilchoman jigsaw (for the time being) was very well received across the board and guests and visitors continue to flock to the distillery to enjoy all the facilities (Over 30,000 in 2023).

During early March 2020 Anthony Wills and Alex Bruce from Ardnamurchan introduced to the market a new bottling called 'KilchArd', a blended malt consisting of one cask from each of the two distilleries. A 2013 Kilchoman bourbon barrel peated at 50 ppm and a Pedro Ximénez sherry cask from Ardnamurchan, peated at 30 ppm, were selected, both from Concerto barley.

The English pronunciation of the name is 'Killhard' and in a nod to the 'Die Hard' series of films, and its star, the surnames of Bruce and Wills were added in bold on the label. A definite step up in marketing was evident here!

The first recorded cases of COVID-19 from Wuhan China were reported in November 2019 and by January 2020 the first case outside China was reported in Thailand. By March 2020, this was declared by the World Health Organisation as a worldwide pandemic. Throughout the UK a lockdown was brought into force on 26 March, creating chaos for businesses. Little did Anthony or his team know what was to follow over the next two years.

Peter was on a stag week in Florida at the time the worldwide problem manifested itself, and he managed to get the last flight out of Florida before the lock down occurred.

James had a new-born baby, living in Edinburgh, and his father suggested at the start of COVID that he move over to Islay with his family, as he wouldn't be able to travel. This made sense in many ways and helped the distillery stay operational when others closed.

They did a series of projections, for a 10% sales drop, 20% sales drop, up to a 60% sales drop, but could have no idea what was about to happen.

Kilchoman was one of the first distilleries to understand what COVID might mean to their business. They didn't over-analyse things and just tried to get content out there on social media at the start of COVID. That involved live sessions on Instagram and Facebook, showcasing the distillery, and showing Anthony and James having a dram, which went down very well with Kilchoman and whisky fans more generally. James, looking back at that first attempt, suggested that his dad spoke like a newsreader and there were one or two issues with wi-fi.

When the first lockdown was implemented, Anthony was concerned as to the future as there were so many imponderables. No-one had any idea how long the lockdown would be in place (although groups of six were allowed to meet up from 28 May, most retail establishments were not allowed to open until 4 July) or what the longer-term implications would be on business.

Kilchoman's marketing team saw some of the potential problems that would come across the next few months, but as with everyone else, did not expect the wider impact of COVID-19 to go on for up to two years, with unrestricted travel to Islay not being allowed by the Scottish government until April 26, 2021 (200,000 visitors come to Islay annually, so the direct impact was significant).

They went into this with a 'Can do' attitude, after James had come up with the original idea of online tastings. It wasn't a question of "Oh we can't do that", it was a question of "How can we make it happen?" There were lots of hurdles to get over, not least the poor wi-fi that Islay is saddled with, but they managed it with resounding success.

Ahead of almost all other distilleries, the marketing team saw an opportunity to sell the Kilchoman brand to a wide market despite the imminent lockdown. On 20 March 2020, Kilchoman invited whisky fans to a 'Friday Night In with Anthony Wills' for the first time. Live on Instagram, Anthony reported on distillery news and in particular on the opening of the new still house and the visitor centre. He answered questions from the online audience, and they all tasted the core range of whiskies sent out in distillery packs.

Judging the response to this first effort a success, more social media content followed immediately and the marketing team felt that they could do a similar thing by selling samples and this proved massively successful. There was a captive audience, of people who wanted to be transported away from the drudgery of their lockdown lives and the new visitor centre at Kilchoman provided that.

The initial core range tasting was followed by one on 27 March – 'Kilchoman Through the Ages', on 03 April, with 'Cask Samples', where 70 tasting packs were sold within minutes.

On 10 April '2020 Limited Releases' went ahead with 200 packs available and sold. This forward thinking enabled regular online tastings to be scheduled, from April 2020 with tasting packs exploring the breadth of the Kilchoman expressions and looking at barley and yeast varieties. To many this was their first experience of Kilchoman, their first look at the new visitor centre and many fell in love with the distillery due to the hard work of the marketing team during this period.

The inability to travel to distributors and retailers, or take the Land Rover to Europe or the USA, to attend whisky fairs and having a closed visitor centre could have been the death knell for a small distillery, but this series of tastings and regular supply of information to a hungry fan base was to have precisely the opposite effect.

What was also not immediately obvious was that the whole population would be sitting at home wanting something to do. Many were furloughed (how many people knew of this word prior to COVID?), but still getting paid and many were working from home, so saving money on the daily commute and coffees. With this, many people had considerably more disposable income, were unable to spend it on holidays, as foreign travel was still not allowed, so they were looking for something to spend their money on. Many spent more time online and as they could not go out for a drink many were purchasing whisky and other alcohol online. Consumption of alcohol increased considerably during lockdown and the word 'Zoom' came into everyday vocabulary.

While the country was in turmoil, Anthony, James, along with Islay Heads, Scott, Derek and Michael were working in a socially distanced manner in the bottling hall, bottling as quickly as the equipment allowed. Whilst everyone else was learning to bake, they were bottling all day every day. The flexibility allowed them to get out single casks, small batches and samples, which was simply not possible at the larger distilleries.

All the larger distilleries at this time felt a responsibility to shut down production, just due to the scale of the businesses and people in contact with each other. Kilchoman, being a smaller operation, could have kept everyone safe in production and therefore could have continued with production, but Anthony and the board did not feel that this was the right thing to do, so they shut the distillery down for six weeks.

After six weeks, Anthony arranged to bring the production team back. He didn't bring back the bottling crew or the visitor centre team until July 2020.

To his surprise, the business, that had been growing at 10/15% per annum, suddenly started growing at 30%, even though the sales team were unable to see anyone in person for two years. Online sales went through the roof during the lockdown periods. The same was probably true across the industry. All the Kilchoman distributors were busy throughout the period.

COVID was initially a very worrying time for Michael Fraser Milne in New Zealand. Whisky Galore works with about 26 distilleries/independent bottlers in Scotland and had, just prior to COVID, brought in a very large shipment. Michael worried about how they were going to pay for this, when Jacinda Ardern closed the borders in New Zealand. He needn't have worried. Due to the sizeable stocks they had purchased, the whisky sold very well and very quickly, to people stuck at home, with additional money in their pockets.

Michael recalls that many of the larger distilleries/companies in Scotland couldn't get staff in to do their bottling/packaging, and one of the few exceptions to this was Kilchoman. There was never a hiccup with Kilchoman, and throughout this period supplies were maintained and even increased.

During COVID, Michael was very impressed with the online presence which Kilchoman introduced before anyone else, and participated in these tastings, even though they were at around 8:00am in New Zealand! He sold 180 packs for one of the tastings. They were so popular that Whisky Galore has carried on with virtual online tastings.

There was a massive rise in the social media interaction, with time being devoted by the team to this most important of outlets. That has continued until today, with videos explaining the different aspects of whisky production by members of each of the teams, updates on what is happening on the farm, sowing and harvesting times.

Whilst the COVID years 2019-2021 saw phenomenal growth in sales, this came with a downside in that the stocks in certain years have taken a battering, specifically the bourbon stocks, due to the increase in Machir Bay sales and to a lesser extent Sanaig.

The Fèis Ìle releases for 2020 and 2021 could only be sold online, rather than solely at the distillery, so Kilchoman substantially expanded the number of available bottles, which all sold (2,630 and 2,832 bottles respectively). Many single casks, which would usually only be available at the distillery, were produced for sale online and all sold very quickly, increasing the throughput of single bottles during 2020 and 2021.

Surprisingly therefore, despite the hardship felt in many quarters, the distilling industry in general and Kilchoman in particular, were one of the few beneficiaries from the Covid outbreak.

Kilchoman's Fèis Ìle 2020 in line with many other distilleries was held remotely with a series of online events, discussions, tastings taking place during 28 May 2020. Despite teething problems with sales of the festival bottles from the shop, due to wi-fi bandwidth issues (an issue seemingly in common with all their Islay neighbours), the day itself was very well received with many being able to experience first-hand, albeit remotely, the joys of festival week.

The Kilchoman virtual Fèis Ìle 2020 also saw the official sales launch of the second limited release of 2020, Am Bùrach. In true Kilchoman fashion they turned what could have been a costly error into a marketing success.

In 2014, due to an operational error, the valves of the two vatting tanks used to marry the casks of the major releases were opened, causing the contents of the two tanks to mix. One was holding a batch of Machir Bay, the other Kilchoman's first port release announced for 2014. Anthony was understandably very upset by this mistake (although I'm not sure his precise response is one that I can publish) so "what a mess!" (or something a little more Anglo-Saxon!) was translated into Gaelic by General Manager Islay Heads as 'Am Bùrach', which sounds much more in keeping with a malt whisky.

Rather than throwing away this involuntary blend, Anthony decided to fill it back into bourbon casks to see how it developed. The Port release in 2014 ended up being a significantly smaller number of bottles.

After 6 years of maturation, Anthony found that the contents of these casks had developed into a thoroughly delicious whisky. To enhance the fruity character, it was then matured for another six months in 100 litre ruby port casks. This shows that the art of blending is never an exact science and luck, bad and good, can play its part.

As a further way of enhancing/creating discussion around the brand, between 28 May and 11 June 2020, there was the first Kilchoman Cask Auction, consisting of five casks, the first sale of casks since 2007 and on the 15th anniversary of opening of the distillery (the official opening being at Fèis Ìle 2005). A total of 15 casks were auctioned in 2020 in three groups of five casks of Kilchoman new make spirit, which achieved prices of between £10,900 for an STR hogshead and £12,500 for an Oloroso hogshead.

Two further auctions with five casks each followed at the end of September/beginning of October and in December 2020. When comparison is made with sales of other new make spirit from similar distilleries, these prices and similar values for the further 10 casks later in the year show that Kilchoman was highly valued relative to other young distilleries.

2021 saw many first releases, with batches of Pedro Ximenez, Tequila and Mezcal being introduced to the market, and all to excellent reviews.

Fèis 2021 in May, saw the same mix of online activities, tastings, discussions, sculpted into an extremely well-crafted day by the marketing team, with similar online tasting packs and festival bottles meeting with less wi-fi resistance this year.

Virtual visitors were also offered a unique opportunity to explore all corners of Kilchoman on Facebook, Instagram and YouTube, through something called '360° Fèis Ìle'.

With a 360° tour, a visitor could use the scroll buttons to enable them to see every corner of the distillery. Members of the Kilchoman team led the viewer on a complete tour of operations, from barley fields to bottling hall, across the courtyard, into the maltings, the still house and the warehouses. Whilst it could never equal the experience of being at a festival, it was an excellent alternative, and for those where distance probably prevented them from ever going to Kilchoman, it was a wonderful way of experiencing the feel of the distillery.

2021 was also notable for the fact that this was the year that the Turnbulls exited the business. As I have discussed, the Turnbulls were largely instrumental, alongside Niels/Moonpal and John Thorogood in saving Kilchoman, at a time when the business could easily have folded. Thankfully they all had the foresight to see what Anthony was trying to do and supported the business and Anthony's vision financially through that difficult time.

According to Anthony, the Turnbulls had always intended to be involved for a certain period before they would look for their exit. They probably stayed longer than they needed to, but have ultimately done well out of the business, as has John Thorogood. When the Turnbulls came to exit the business, they looked at options to sell their 30% stake, but as this was a minority stake in the business, it was unlikely that any major player would want to take it on.

The logical thing to do would be to sell their stake to Moonpal. The Turnbulls had always indicated that they saw Anthony and his family as integral to the business and they fully supported Anthony and his management team.

Moonpal, who would then be the significant majority shareholder and could have voted any matters through without Anthony's agreement, saw that this would create a perhaps insurmountable problem for the Wills family, so he indicated he was prepared to make a change to the Articles of Association of the business, to give Anthony confidence that he couldn't lose his share of the business if Moonpal decided to sell. As they had worked together for the last 12 years, it seemed sensible for the Turnbulls to sell their shares to Moonpal, so that Anthony could continue with the excellent working relationship they had built up.

To complete the circle, in 2022, John Thorogood sold his shares, representing 9% of the business, also to Moonpal. Currently there are two main shareholders, the Wills family with just under 25%, a couple of small shareholders, with just over 1%, with Moonpal owning the rest. There are board meetings with Moonpal and Niels four times a year, they speak every month to discuss how things are progressing, but generally, Anthony is allowed to get on with the running of the business. George, Peter and James also attend all the board meetings.

One of the issues not apparent during the first year or so of the COVID pandemic, was that some consumables would become hard to source. This was especially true of glass and during the latter part of 2021, Kilchoman had to postpone the release of the first Madeira cask batch as they didn't have sufficient bottles to complete the bottling. This was to become a major issue during 2021 and beyond throughout the industry.

2022 saw another first. Kilchoman marketing team had recognised the importance, especially during the COVID years of online marketing. The Kilchoman Appreciation Society on Facebook has over 5,000 members and the distillery agreed to produce a single cask bottle for the Society. Fifty fortunate members tasted four different cask samples in an online tasting with Anthony on 3 February 2022 and chose Sauternes Cask No. 903/2015, which was subsequently bottled and sold by the distillery.

Fèis Île 2022, saw visitors return for the festival for the first time in three years. It was a celebration of all things good about the distillery. Visitors were able to see first-hand the developments that had been made over the previous three years, not least the expansion of the visitor centre, which contained many of Kathy Wills' touches within the design of her sister Nicola and will serve the distillery well for many years into the future.

The collaboration with Ardnamurchan continued to a second joint bottling in 2022 to celebrate the 175th anniversary of the Glenalmond College in Perthshire, comprising a peated cask of Kilchoman from 2014 and an unpeated cask of Ardnamurchan from 2015.

The connection is that George, James and Peter Wills of Kilchoman and Alex Bruce of Adelphi/Ardnamurchan are all former Glenalmond students. 553 bottles of the Glenalmond 175 blended malt were bottled at 52.0% and the proceeds from the sale of each bottle were donated to Glenalmond to fund scholarships.

As part of their marketing plan, 2023 saw the relaunch of the European Land Rover tour. After a break of five years, and following on from the tours in 2014, 2015 and 2018, the Kilchoman Land Rover and trailer once again headed across Europe, dispensing Kilchoman to the masses.

The tour crossed 13 countries, with events ranging from store led afternoon tastings to extensive evening tastings, with the Kilchoman Land Rover arriving back on Islay for Fèis Ìle at the end of May. The whole of the Kilchoman marketing and sales team were involved in these events at some stage. George, James, Peter, Carol-Ann MacTaggart, Chloe Wood, Catherine MacMillan and Antea Allegro all saw some of the sights Europe had to offer.

As Rabbie Burns so eloquently expressed it, "The best laid schemes o'mice an'men gang aft agley." As with all best laid plans, there needs to be a Plan B. When the Land Rover broke down in Germany, the replacement was a non-Kilchoman transit van, which didn't have the same romantic appeal as driving a liveried Land Rover round the drinking dens of Europe. George and James ended up doing the UK leg in George's car, normally half an hour later than they were supposed to arrive due to some mishap or other along the way.

In the latter part of 2024, the Kilchoman team undertook a Far East tour, with Anthony joining Peter and other members of the marketing and sales teams in China and South Korea. It is the first time Anthony has been to China since his independent bottling days in the late 1990's.

Immediately after the Far East tour the team led by James, went on a US tour visiting 50 US outlets over several weeks, concluding an exceptionally busy year for the marketing and sales team.

Chapter 10

The Future

Kilchoman is still a relatively small brand and there are untapped markets out there. Whisky sales have grown significantly over the last six or seven years, be it through an expansion in whisky drinking throughout the mature and developing world, or through collectors, generally at the higher end of the market. The last 12 months or so has seen sales across the industry declining and a contraction in the market generally, although there are signs that this may be levelling out, certainly as far as Kilchoman is concerned.

There is still opportunity for expansion in areas like USA, Europe, Far East and Australasia. There is also an untapped market for brands like Kilchoman in India and China for example, where there is a rapidly growing middle class with higher disposable income and tariffs/barriers to trade are being removed for the scotch whisky industry.

Expansion into rum in Barbados is another major step. The rum distillery was Peter's idea, and the board was fully supportive. This is an attempt to premiumise another quality spirit, using quality sugar cane, and a similar template to the success they had achieved at Kilchoman.

Nine acres of land and the derelict house at Bentley Mansion were purchased in the Parish of St. Philip in August 2021. The plan is to erect buildings to house the distillery, mill and cask warehouse, purchase sugar cane from the fields surrounding Bentley Mansion, crush it on site and produce rum from sugar cane juice and cane syrup in two copper pot stills followed by maturation and bottling on site.

There is a history of distilling in Barbados, other distillers are still on the island, and Kilchoman has already had many conversations with the likes of Richard Seale at Four Square, Alexandre Gabriel at Plantation Rum and Mount Gay, all of whom are well-established rum brands.

There is some frustration as Kilchoman has been trying to progress this project for several years (they had an initial visit in 2015), but bureaucracy has often got in the way of their development. However, this has also given them the time to get to know people in Barbados and for those locally to realise that this is a genuine venture, which will bring increased prosperity and jobs to the island, should it ever go ahead.

Kilchoman also want to produce a strict set of Geographical Indications (GI), which would involve distilling, maturing, and bottling on the island to help create a Barbadian (Bajan) brand. A distillery cannot miss out one of those component parts and still be part of the GI. It seems unlikely that this will happen, as other producers do their own thing. For example, Alexandre Gabriel of Plantation Rum doesn't live on Barbados, although he visits regularly. He ships all the casks back to Cognac, where he lives, for maturation.

Anthony has enlisted Frank Ward, former Mount Gay Managing Director, who will be consulting on the project and advising on specific rum production methods. This will offer a combination of existing expertise in single malt whisky production and Mr Ward's vast knowledge in rum production.

Kilchoman had two previous attempts to get something off the ground locally, working with partners, without success. They are employing a quantity surveyor in Barbados to do the build work.

Planning permission has been obtained, although it took until March 2023 to be granted, the intention was that tenders would be sought, and contractors reviewed. However, due to much higher interest rates and the downturn in the whisky industry since 2023, this has been put on hold. The hope is that this is temporary, but it would be foolish to progress when interest rates were high and market sentiment towards premium spirits had declined a little. The project has been driven forward by Peter, and in the event it goes ahead, he will be spending time out there whilst it is being built and to ensure that the initial production goes well.

The initial intention was for at a 12-month site build followed by the installation of stills, with the aspiration of being in production late 2024/early 2025. Clearly this will not now happen. Due to the much higher temperatures in the Caribbean, maturation of the spirit will be a great deal quicker than maturing whisky on Islay. Islay cannot claim the number of sunny days nor does it have anywhere near the average year-round temperature that its Caribbean counterpart boasts. The rum distillery should be able to produce a rum within two years, with peak maturation likely to be five to eight years, as and when they recommence this project.

Kilchoman is well supported by Barclays now, who are committed to the rum project, as and when it gets off the ground and the expansion of the whisky distillery. It is much easier to convince banks to lend you money when you have the depth of inventory that Kilchoman is now carrying.

With a significant increase in new distilleries coming online in the last few years and in the next four or five years it will be interesting to see how the market reacts and whether there is enough capacity out there to embrace all of these. It seems very unlikely to me and already there is evidence of issues throughout the industry with the closure of Waterford, Penderyn ceasing production and many distilleries reducing their production levels for the time being.

Locally, Kilchoman received planning permission from Argyll and Bute Council for another five warehouses over the next eight years or so, planning is so important to the development of the distillery.

The next challenge is that Diageo have indicated that their Port Ellen maltings, from where many of the Islay distilleries have traditionally sourced their peated malt, will not supply anyone other than Diageo distilleries (Caol Ila, Lagavulin and Port Ellen on Islay) from 2024. The main obstacle that this introduces is that the increase in ferry traffic needed to bring that additional amount of malted barley onto the island would swamp the current ferry system. (Port Ellen currently brings its barley in by a separate vessel every couple of weeks).

Kilchoman has put in planning permission to build its own maltings. Anthony believes that peating of the malt on Islay, using Islay peat is important for their brand. They have recognised the issues that will become apparent for all Islay distilleries from 2024 and are trying to be proactive. They have engaged with a contractor experienced in carrying out builds within the brewing industry across the world (recently completing one in America). There are at present discussions taking place between other Islay distilleries and Baird's Malt, about building a maltings on Islay, but there is no certainty that this would ever come to fruition.

Beam Suntory, LVMH and Distell are having those discussions, but it would be necessary to put in a pier, and a road, to a location beyond Bunnahabhain. Islay Estates are also involved, as they own a forest behind

Bunnahabhain, but currently have no way of harvesting the wood and getting it out. Kilchoman has been provided with a copy of the papers and have been involved in these discussions. The pre-planning application would be £70/80,000. The cost of upgrading the pier and road could be £7/8m, so a significant expense, just to bring in barley, albeit in time there could possibly be a range of products that could be brought in via this route.

The intention of the other distilleries would be to bring in malted barley and then apply peat to it, hoping that the particles will cling to the dry grain. Anthony's view of that is that with moving the barley from silo to lorry to silo, the particles will rub off, so his preference would be to malt and peat on site.

Logistically, it will be quite a challenge to bring the barley onto Islay, because of the ferry issues. There are currently 35 loads of malted barley coming onto Islay per week. The carbon footprint of bringing regular lorry loads of barley is another issue. Kilchoman sees the answer as bringing in ship loads of malted barley onto the island and storing it in silos until needed. Discussions are ongoing in relation to this, and it will be interesting to see if a more permanent solution can be found, as the issues with the ferries are well documented and significantly more tankers using the ferries will create massive problems.

Being conscious of other environmental issues, and the impact of tankers on the roads, the company are looking at a digester to dispose of all their effluent on site.

Kilchoman had plans to put in two more sets of stills, a bigger mash tun (3.5 tonnes) and 18,000 litre washbacks, originally due for completion by the end of 2024. These plans have been put on hold until market conditions recover sufficiently to justify the additional production. With the additional stills, mash tun and washbacks, production capacity will go up to 1.3 million litres.

Chapter 11

Technical (Geeky Stuff)

At the outset in 2005, Kilchoman really was a distillery on a micro scale. When the distillery first produced spirit in 2005, there was a 3,230 litre wash still, a 2,070 litre spirit still, a 1.2 tonne mash tun, four 6000 litre stainless steel washbacks, kiln and malting floor, visitor centre and café, but no bottling hall. At that time there was a single warehouse.

In 2007 two more washbacks were fitted and two further warehouses were built.

A new bottling room was completed in 2011.

New warehousing was built at Consiby, near Bruichladdich, along with a second warehouse at Kilchoman in 2013. In the same year a heat exchanger was fitted and further additions made to the bottling room.

Two new vatting tanks were installed in 2014 in Warehouse 1, improvements to the malt transport system added and a cork applying machine and conveyors were introduced to the bottling hall.

2017 saw the construction of a new kiln and malting floor, doubling the capacity of malting local barley to four tonnes per week.

In the significant expansion of 2019, there was the extension from the gable end of the stillhouse to effectively form a new still house with an identical wash and spirit still added to the originals, an additional mash tun and six new stainless steel washbacks, making 14 in total. A much larger visitor centre, café and shop was also constructed.

Finally in 2020 a second mash tun was fitted.

Kilchoman plans to put in two more sets of stills, a bigger mash tun (3.5 tonnes) and 18,000 litre washbacks, but this has now been put on hold until market conditions recover. There is also a programmed expansion of the warehousing from the current six warehouses, over the next few years.

Kilchoman is one of only a handful of distilleries still practising traditional floor malting, a process that most of Scotland's distilleries have outsourced to commercial maltsters. The labour-intensive nature of floor malting is a significant factor in its demise, though it remains at the heart of Kilchoman's philosophy. The 100% Islay represents the revival of traditional farm distilling, standing alone as Islay's only single farm, single malt scotch whisky, completing all stages of the process at Kilchoman from barley to bottle.

The concept of a farm distillery and using local barley is within Anthony's DNA. As the distillery grows in terms of production, the amount of locally grown barley will reduce, unless they take steps to increase that production. Rockside farm comprises 2,300 acres surrounding the ruined Kilchoman Church. Much of the land is unsuitable for growing barley and is grazed by sheep and cattle.

The most fertile ground, currently around 400 acres of rich soil surrounding the distillery, is reserved for the annual barley crop. In 2022 Islay Head's team completed the draining of one field, which is being brought into production, and two further fields are in planning (without adequate drainage, these fields would be too wet to grow barley to the production levels that the distillery needs). There are currently 12 fields on which barley is grown in rotation.

The distillery must wait until 30,000 barnacle geese and 5,500 Greenland white-fronted geese have departed in April before sowing the barley, as they would eat everything that was sown. The intention is to increase annual barley production over the next couple of years to the region of 400 tonnes, but ultimately it is never likely to be more than 25% of their whisky production. In 2008, only 15 years ago, the production was 100 tonnes, so a lot more of the farmland has been brought into barley production.

The production for the 2023 season was approximately 273 tonnes over 155 acres sowed with Sassy and Planet varieties of barley, in 2024 it was LG Diablo and Laureate sowed over the same acreage, which produced 321 tonnes of barley, enough to fill 800 barrels with new make spirit. Laureate is the highest yielding variety of spring barley available in Scotland and the team have experimented with it over a few years to see how it compared in terms of both yield and balance of flavour profile. It is readily used in the country for malting and brewing and continues to be one of the top performers.

LG Diablo is a newer variety which was approved for use in malting in 2019, with the first crop being grown on the farm in 2020. Having used it for a few years now they remain very happy with how it performs throughout production. In prior years they have used Optic, Chalice and Publican.

Malting consists of three main functions: steeping, germinating and kilning. As the first of these steps, steeping could be said to be the most critical. The process of steeping determines final malt quality and if Kilchoman doesn't get this stage right, there is a greater chance of problems later in the malting stage.

At Kilchoman, the harvested barley can be stored for up to a year before being steeped. The purpose of steeping is to 'awaken' the barley and trigger germination by achieving an optimal moisture level in the grain which is normally between 43% and 45%. The three main considerations at this stage are temperature, moisture content and germination, which are all carefully monitored by the team throughout.

The steeping regimes vary at different times of the year to ensure optimal conditions are maintained. For example, in the colder winter months they often use an eight-hour steeping cycle following which the barley is drained and left for another eight hours before repeating these steps for a total of three cycles. In the warmer months they complete 12-hour steeping cycles after which the barley is drained and left for 12 hours before repeating whole process again, so only two cycles in the summer. Both cycles take a total time of 48 hours, the significant difference is the water temperature during each steep. Ideally, Kilchoman wants a temperature of between 12° and 16° Celsius.

In the summer the temperature outside rises as does the temperature of the water sourced from nearby Gleann Osamail. The shorter eight-hour steeping time across three steeps helps Kilchoman maintain a cooler water. Barley steeped at warmer temperatures develops less a-amylase enzymes which are critical for mashing. Another benefit of using colder steep water and a longer steep cycle is that there is a more uniform water uptake and hydration throughout the kernel.

As well as ensuring the correct ambient temperature throughout, the right combinations of water and air must be provided to ensure the moisture content of the grain is raised to the required level of around 43-45%, without 'drowning' it!

Typically, the first soak will bring the moisture level up to only around 37% so further steeping is required. By using multiple watering, the air rest time after each steep allows the grain to accept more water in the next steep. It also avoids the risk that the grain will become saturated resulting in slower chitting if too much water is added too quickly. The precise mechanics of the operation have been honed and perfected over centuries.

It is crucial that the moisture content of the germinating barley is distributed as evenly as possible between each kernel. Air is blown through the grain between the wet phases to remove carbon dioxide and toxic metabolites, to discharge excess heat and to replenish oxygen as well as helping to ensure that the grains are all modifying in a consistent way.

During steeping, hydration stimulates the embryo into growth and respiration commences. If unchecked, the heat generated during steeping as the grain respires has a cumulative effect and forces the grain to respire more rapidly. Uncontrolled respiration causes the grain to hydrate quicker but in an irregular fashion throughout the grain population which can cause problems.

At around 35% moisture content the embryo within each kernel of barley will start to germinate, but there is insufficient moisture to allow the complete modification of the starchy endosperm that Kilchoman requires. Reaching the desired moisture level during steeping and later at the drying stage is crucial as it determines the quality of the malt and will have an impact on the overall yield.

When the desired moisture content of between 43-45% is reached the 'green malt' (the term for the barley at this stage) is spread on the malt floor by hand using traditional methods for the second phase of growth.

The thickness of the green malt spread on the floor is a judgment the team makes in order to maintain the ambient conditions. In the colder months the room temperature will be lower, so the green malt is spread more thickly in a layer 400-500mm deep. In comparison, during the warmer times of the year the green malt is spread more thinly, and they open windows to help cool the room. The reason for this is to maintain the ambient grain temperature to allow growing to continue. During particularly cold spells, the malting team have had occasion to keep the door from the kiln area open to gain some extra heat from the kiln fire.

Throughout germination it is essential that the grain bed maintains moisture otherwise the grain could become dehydrated and result in restricted modification. The moisture of the grain is monitored throughout to maintain a moisture content above 40%.

Ensuring there is a sufficient supply of oxygen to the grain whilst also maintaining an even temperature throughout all the grains is also vital. To guarantee there is adequate aeration and an even temperature the barley is turned every four hours by hand using traditional tools.

Two major changes occur during the time the green malt is on the floor: firstly, enzymes are developed which break down the cell walls, the action of these enzymes provides freely available starch. Secondly, other enzymes are produced which break down proteins. Further enzymes are developed which will convert the starch into fermentable sugars in the mash tun during the mashing stage. These changes are known as 'modification'. When the acrospire (sprout) is visibly around three quarters the length of the grain, this indicates that the time has come to stop the germination process and conserve the enzymes required for mashing. It takes around five days to get to this stage.

If germination continued a plant would grow and all the starches that convert to alcohol during fermentation would be used by the plant. The kilning stage terminates germination and prevents this from happening by reducing the moisture content of the green malt.

From the malt floor, the green malt is moved by hand to a conveyor which transfers it to the kiln. To obtain the peat smoke character in Kilchoman, peat is cut locally and burns under controlled conditions for approximately 10-15 hours. During this time the peat smoke rises through the mesh kiln floor and penetrates the green malt. Peating the barley for this period gives it a phenolic level of approximately 20 parts per million (ppm). The barley is then used to make the 100% Islay. All other products (apart from a short run of 'unpeated' barley) use barley which is peated to 50ppm and was purchased through Port Ellen Maltings until the end of 2024.

There are three main variables that affect the kilning process: temperature, airflow and time. A combination of high moisture and high temperature would destroy the enzymes developed during germination therefore the production team maintains a low temperature to avoid this. Rather than a roaring kiln fire, it is controlled so that it smoulders, as they are looking to produce as much smoke from the peat as possible but keep the temperature inside the kiln from getting too hot.

Like when the green malt is on the floor, maintaining an appropriate and even temperature as well as good aeration is vital so turning by hand will continue every few hours and the temperature inside the kiln is monitored and adapted as required.

Following on from the 10 -15 hours of peating, the production team continue to reduce the moisture content for a further 20 hours approximately by forcing air through the green malt until it reaches a moisture content of 4.7-5%. The kilned product is now called malt and is in a stable form. The grain is dormant and can now be transferred to rest in the silos for a minimum of six weeks before being milled for mashing.

Milling takes place through a Porteus Patent Malt Mill which has been running consistently for eighty years, previously at a brewery in Yorkshire, before being purchased by Kilchoman. This mill is much smaller than those at other distilleries on Islay, but as with all Porteus Mills, it has stood the test of time.

The mill is used to expose the sugars from within the tough outer husk of the barley grains, with the barley ending up as grist, a mix of husk, grit, and fine flour.

After milling, 1.2 tonnes of grist is transferred to the mash tun. To extract the sugars, the team adds three streams of hot water at 56°C, 85°C and 95°C. 6000 litres of sugary liquid, or wort, goes into the stainless steel washbacks (Jim Swan was a firm believer that Oregon Pine washbacks added nothing to the process and were more difficult to clean), to which is added 20kg of dry yeast. This wort is then left to ferment for approximately 84 hours to become wash, a strong beer at 6-8% abv.

After the barley is grown, harvested, malted, peated, dried, mashed and fermented, it's finally ready for the process of distillation. The first stage is to add the wash from the previous step into a large pot still called the wash still, containing up to 3230 litres. The still is handmade from copper and heated from below, vaporising the liquid into a fine mist, which rises up the neck of the still where it condenses into a liquid historically known as 'low wines', at around 25% alcohol by volume (abv). At Kilchoman, 3000 litres of wash is pumped into the wash still, from this only 1000 litres will become low wines, the rest is pot ale (which is used as fertiliser on their barley fields.)

Since the low wines themselves are not palatable, the still team moves the liquid into a second, smaller still called the spirit still. The spirit still is the smaller of the two, and the most important when it comes to creating the fundamental flavours that define a whisky. The neck shape is a key component, as is the overall size. Kilchoman uses a 2070 litre still with a relatively tall, narrow neck. This is remarkably small compared to some distilleries which are home to pot stills over ten times the size. The Kilchoman spirit still has a tall, narrow neck and the production team distils slowly producing their unique light floral spirit.

The reflux bulb (or boil bulb) on the still aids the purification of the spirit. This is where vapour can circulate and interact with the copper for longer, removing more unwanted compounds and resulting in a more defined flavour. The spirit must work harder to climb up the neck, which creates a clean, light and fruity spirit. Therefore, the larger the reflux bulb the lighter and fresher the spirit will be. There is no right or wrong, with each distillery looking to create their own unique whisky profile, steeped in the traditions of their region.

When heated, the alcohol rises and separates out into three phases of which only the middle phase (or cut) is deemed good enough to be collected for maturation.

Kilchoman spirit runs through a spirit safe and is cut early, from 75% abv to 65.5% abv with the 'heart' being an average of 70%, and this is reduced to 63.5% with water from Gleann Osamail burn before being piped to Kilchoman's filling store to be discharged into casks for maturation in one of the four dunnage warehouses. Meanwhile, the early (foreshots) and late (feints) phases are mixed into the next batch of low wines ready for another round of distillation. From the initial 3000 litres of wash, only 300 litres of new make spirit is created.

Copper is a very important factor when it comes to the pot stills. The interaction between the copper and the liquid will purify the spirit, it will purify the low wines from the wash still and the spirit from the spirit still. The copper component has a heavy influence in producing the end-product of Kilchoman new make spirit. In fact, some pot stills are shaped to maximise copper contact at key points, with the belief that the flavour can be tweaked at just the right level. Copper is also a fine heat conductor, helping to distribute heat evenly.

The art of perfecting the cut requires intimate knowledge of the ingredients involved, from the malted barley to the spring water. Cut too early or late and the impurities of the feints can throw off the balance of whisky. The pot stills may be surrounded by science, but this aspect of the distilling process is a very human art form. It's why expertise and tradition go a long way in creating the best whiskies. As Islay Heads, the Distillery Manager at Kilchoman said, "Tradition makes the whisky, people make the spirit."

Chapter 12

Kilchoman Brand and Products

B rand has always been seen as incredibly important to Anthony and the logo, bottle and packaging made up a significant part of the brand.

I mentioned earlier that Anthony owned a company called Caledonian Selection in the years prior to establishing Kilchoman and Craig Mackinlay had worked with Anthony at that time on some single cask labels. It was he that put the design together for the Kilchoman logo and the bottle and all the packaging.

The bottle is designed to be heavy and chunky, to feel good in the hand, but it's not like other Islay bottles. They wanted to retain some of the look of the 'off the shelf' bottles used in the earliest bottlings, especially the half-moon shaped shoulder, from the label to the neck of the bottle, which lent itself well to the Kilchoman 'coin' being inserted into the shoulder area.

Anthony admits he wasn't creative as far as product design was concerned. All he wanted was a unique bottle, which someone could immediately identify as Kilchoman (many new distilleries are now making sure that their bottles and packaging stand out from the plethora of new releases – see White Peak and Raasay distilleries as great examples of superior modern design).

Price was not particularly a governing factor at the time. The whisky was intended to be at the premium end of the market. The packaging therefore became really important. The extra 52p at the time to put the coin into the neck was seen as money well spent. Originally, releases all had different coins identifying the type of release, but this was stopped around 2016, as it was becoming more and more expensive to do. The coin is now standard on all bottles, much to the dismay of the many 'coin' collectors.

Craig's aim has never been to win design awards, but with his commercial hat on he is intent on making the biggest commercial impact for his client and by his design help his client to sell their product more easily. In his obviously biased (but nevertheless correct) view the design still looks great today and he is proud of his contribution to the success of the Kilchoman brand.

Anthony feels that the whisky should speak for itself and therefore all whiskies are non-chill filtered and with no added colour. The bottles were never going to be anything other than clear glass, unlike other distilleries on Islay. He felt there was nothing to hide and wanted people to be able to look at the colour of the whisky they were pouring as part of the customer experience. The golden hues of a bourbon cask for example contrast beautifully with the dark plum colour of a port cask, enhancing the overall experience.

The split label on the front of the bottle was another deliberate design feature. When they commenced production, the colour palate had been agreed – the Kilchoman blue is Pantone 293. The top label on the bottles was the Kilchoman logo with 'Islay's farm distillery' proudly displayed and the differentiator was the bottom label which explained the bottle contents – Autumn 2009 Release etc.

It was impossible to completely future proof what was going to happen when they looked at this back in 2008. Now Kilchoman produces a wide range of different whiskies, with individual labelling and colouring moving away from the original intention to have the top label in Pantone 293. At that time in 2008 they were looking maybe five years ahead, but the labelling has altered significantly in terms of colour and how the different casks are identified. Inevitably the process evolved as the distillery grew bigger. Machir Bay is the product that has retained that Pantone 293, but there is now a kaleidoscope of colours across the Kilchoman spectrum of whiskies.

The colouration of the boxes followed the colours of the labels. Loch Gorm is a very dark peated loch and hence the colour chosen for the Loch Gorm label and box was black. Machir Bay was a bright blue as befits Machir Bay on a sunny day for anyone who has been there. Sanaig has a light purple colour in keeping with the heavier sherry influence, and port cask releases are in a burgundy/plum colour. Craig's view is that they have tried to keep some vague correlation between the whisky or the name of the whisky and the packaging, although that is more difficult when you get to more modern finishes like Mezcal and Tequila. Presently those are just single cask examples so come with red packaging.

If it had been anticipated in 2008 that there would be such a range of whiskies at Kilchoman, then they would have designed a whole colour pallete for the range. This, by necessity, has evolved as new whiskies have been brought on track. But people associate Machir Bay with blue packaging, Sanaig with purple, Loch Gorm with black, so that will not change at any time in the foreseeable future. However, there has been some tweaking of the labelling with some of the more recent releases, for example, the Sanaig Cask Strength, is a darker plum colour, with a different top label. It was inevitable that the branding would develop as the distillery and the range developed.

Bramble Liqueur had for many years been one of Kilchoman's best-selling products, but it came about purely by chance. Anthony knew the team at the Scottish Liqueur Centre, where Kenny Mackay was working. Kenny has been in the industry for many years and Anthony's relationship with him was longstanding.

Anthony thought it might be a good idea in the early days of Kilchoman to provide something different and sent up some new make spirit for Kenny to mix with their various recipes for single malt honey liqueur. They plumped for one and decided to put it out to the market as an additional way of selling the brand. The smoky, peaty character in the liqueur, balanced well with the brambles and honey.

They started producing Bramble Liqueur when they just had the visitor centre and had commenced making spirit. It was introduced to the public at Fèis 2008. With no whisky yet being bottled, the Bramble Liqueur along with some independent bottlings from Anthony's previous career were vital sources of income. Initially the liqueur was just for sale in the shop, but then they were asked for it round the world, so they increased supply and sent it out to wider markets.

Kilchoman stopped bottling it in 2022. Consideration was given to making the liqueur in house, but at the time, with other expansion plans, this was something which would have created significant logistical issues. Whilst it remains a product that the team remembers fondly and they will not dismiss the possibility of bringing it back, for the time being, it is no longer produced.

In 2012 Machir Bay became Kilchoman's first annual release. Whilst the distillery had been producing the limited releases, they needed core expressions, available all the time and distributors wanted something that they could permanently list. Anthony firmly believes that a distillery cannot grow a brand by releasing small batches and limited editions, core products are needed, and Machir Bay was the first of these. Excellent first year sales of around 15,000 bottles were achieved, growing exponentially over the next ten years to nearly 200,000 bottles. Those sales numbers have been outstripped by Sanaig, which sells around 250,000 bottles.

Machir Bay and Sanaig and the more recently introduced Batch Strength (which will be part of the core range going forward) are building the brand and behind that Kilchoman has the limited releases of Loch Gorm, 100% Islay, and the various wine and fortified wine casks, which are between 8,000 and 20,000 bottles each release. Other more exotic releases will follow in time.

The key also to the future of the brand is pricing. Machir Bay and Sanaig are priced at a point where they are not the cheapest, but Anthony understands that if the price is constantly hiked up, potential customers will look away at something more reasonably priced. Machir Bay was originally priced just below £40 when it was released in 2012. More than ten years later it is still sub-£50 in most retail outlets.

The first sherried release was in 2013, which was the first Loch Gorm. This was the one that was bottled as Sherry Cask, before the idea of calling it Loch Gorm was conceived. That has been a massive success. Anthony confesses that along with the rest of the market, he did not anticipate the explosion of sherried whiskies that occurred around 2018/2019, but he always wanted a high quality sherried whisky as part of the Kilchoman core range.

There is a challenge with sherry and peated whisky, which is getting the balance right. Anthony acknowledges that Bunnahabhain has done a terrific job with sherried whiskies in its Moine range. He wanted to see if it would work with the Kilchoman spirit and had originally been assured by Jim Swan that it would, and this was later confirmed by John Maclellan when he came on board.

The establishment of the Kilchoman Club was essentially following what others in the market were doing. Fans of Kilchoman want access to that special bottling. The first club bottling was in 2012 and 2024 saw the 13th edition of the Club bottling. In the early days it was to allow those relatively low numbers of people to get something special from the distillery. This group has expanded appreciably since its conception, currently there are 30,000 members and at some point, it may become unsustainable.

Originally at the distillery, the mix of casks filled was 70% bourbon and 30% sherry, with 'experimental' casks in addition. Such has been the success of the sherried whiskies, particularly Sanaig, which outsells Machir Bay, that there is now a significantly higher quantity of sherry casks being purchased, so the split is now around 60/40 in favour of bourbon.

The distillery uses mainly sherry butts (approx. 475-500 litres of liquid or 302-350 litres of pure alcohol), although Sanaig, uses solely sherry hogsheads (approx. 225-250 litres of liquid or 142-175 LPA). The reasoning behind this is that the hogshead has more liquid in contact with the wood, which gives off a much stronger sherry influence, hence some of the Sanaig releases, where the casks have been exceptionally active, can be very dark, whilst others are much lighter. Either way there is a stronger sherry influence in a shorter time than will be achieved from a butt.

Loch Gorm in sherry butts, is more balanced, whereas Sanaig provides a big sherry hit. The issue, in a good way for Kilchoman, is that Sanaig is loved more than Machir Bay. As the distillery develops and more people are drinking Kilchoman products, the cask maturation philosophy evolves and will continue to do so in line with consumer demands.

Late in 2017 was the first red wine release. In the early years Anthony worked closely with Jim Swan and with his help, was put in touch with the J Dias cooperage in Portugal, who supplied a lot of the experimental casks, mainly Madeira, Port, STR casks and red wines from Portugal. These are strongly flavoured red wines, so the flavours leach into the casks, which are gradually drawn out during the maturation and provide those strong red fruit notes to the whisky.

Jim was of the belief that Kilchoman's spirit would work with stronger flavours and higher alcohol strength wines and fortified wines. Anthony believes that the Kilchoman spirit reacts better with fortified wines than still wines and the Madeira cask 2021 is a great example of that.

Kilchoman wants to be transparent about the types of casks they use and would willingly put on full details of the vineyards and the type of grape/wine that the cask previously held. The simple truth is that many of the Chateaux will not allow details of their high-quality wine to be displayed on the bottle of what they perceive might be an inferior whisky, thus not enhancing their brand. It is simpler to refuse to give permission for the details to be displayed. Over time, Anthony hopes to convince some, if not all, of the vineyards/chateaux to allow details of their casks to be displayed on Kilchoman whisky. For the time being, it will be a more generic term seen on the bottle.

The production of a whisky called 'Comraich' was another important step (and marketing tool) for Kilchoman. This whisky was supplied to partner bars throughout the world but limited to the bars and not for outside sale, although that line appears to have become blurred, especially during COVID when bars could not sell any whisky direct and to cover costs were forced to sell on stock.

Comraich is Gaelic and means 'sanctuary' or 'asylum'. In Scotland during medieval times, sanctuary sites were commonplace. During those years, if you had debts, you could face a prison sentence or, in more extreme cases, death. But if you were able to make your way to a sanctuary site, you could live there indefinitely without fear of your creditors.

Sanctuary sites were marked by four cornerstones that were placed one Scottish mile (the length of the Royal Mile in Edinburgh – 1.8km) out from a central point. In most cases, that was a church or place of worship.

On Islay, one such site was located close to the old parish church at Kilchoman, and one of the remaining stones marked with a cross is still very much visible today. One of the other stones now rests at the Islay Museum, where it was taken to be protected. The presence of these cross marked stones denotes that this was a very important area in medieval times.

Sanctuary sites carried on in Scotland until 1880, when an act of parliament meant that debtors could no longer be jailed, but many of the markers to guide you to those old sites still exist. Like the one on Islay, or more famously, the gold S slabs on the grounds of Holyrood Palace in Scotland's capital city.

According to Kilchoman, finding a place of 'Comraich' allows us to relax and forget all our troubles and enjoy a dram of Kilchoman. This was the idea behind the Comraich global network of bars (around 180), dedicated to the enjoyment of their single malt, with exclusive releases to sample – details of the bars can be found on the Kilchoman website, I managed to find my way to one such bar, Baxters when I was in Sydney and it was everything I had hoped it would be.

To date there have been seven releases of Comraich, all containing a different mix of casks. The first was bourbon and oloroso sherry, second was purely bourbon, third 100% Islay bourbon and oloroso sherry, fourth bourbon, fifth fresh port, sixth Calvados and the 2024 edition being 100% Islay ex-bourbon casks.

From 2018 to 2020, Kilchoman offered certain whisky retailers a 'Machir Bay Collaborative Vatting', which is a variation on the standard Machir Bay.

Ordinarily, Machir Bay bottlings would have an Oloroso sherry cask content of around 10%, but with a Collaborative Vatting, the retailer has four options with slightly different proportions of sherry - 5%, 7.5%, 12.5% and 15%. The boxes and bottles in the normal Machir Bay design are provided with the name of the retailer added. During COVID this product was no longer supplied.

This has certainly helped to establish the Kilchoman brand to the market, especially in the USA. This has largely been superseded by the Small Batch Releases, which are targeted at specific countries/markets rather than one distributor. The Small Batches are bourbon and sherry plus another type of cask. Kilchoman is now providing larger volumes of the Small Batches for customers that want them.

These all add to the range, providing a twist to the traditional supply and have been extremely well received. This innovation came from the marketing team talking to distributors who asked for something slightly different at a different price point.

Kilchoman has been forced to cap the number of single casks that they will release in a year – somewhere around 180 – because they simply do not have the time to be continually changing the bottling line. Many distilleries do not produce single cask offerings, for that very reason, but Kilchoman sees this as an integral part of their offering.

Kilchoman is an innovative distillery, providing an environment for all their staff to contribute towards the continued development of the distillery. All suggestions are considered and many of them acted upon by a management team keen to continue with the distillery's expansion and reach into the market.

In conclusion and by way of answering the question that I posed on the cover of the book, I think Kilchoman remains at heart a farm distillery. The ethos they have as a business, trying to employ locally, growing as much barley as the land on Islay will allow, so that up to 30% of their whisky now and in the future will be 100% Islay, caring for the environment in which the distillery sits, and continuing to operate the farm as it was run previously, all point to the fact that this is a farm distillery.

On the flip side, Anthony had always intended to keep this as a small-scale operation, and it was his sons joining the business that effectively determined the plans to expand. In a year or two Kilchoman may well be producing 1.3m litres of alcohol a year, which would seem to take it beyond the realms of a farm distillery. Perhaps there is not a simple answer, but to me Kilchoman will never have the feel of anything other than a farm distillery. I leave you to make your own informed judgment, but would urge you, if you can, go to the distillery, which will help you make that judgment. A typical Islay welcome is sure to greet you if you do.

There is no doubt, however that the decision of the three boys to join the business has meant that there is now a family legacy and from what I have seen, the future of the distillery is in very good hands, just waiting for the next generation.

I wish to express my thanks to Anthony, Kathy, George, James and Peter for their assistance in putting together this book, along with many other people at the distillery, distributors and contractors, who have all helped me get a sense of the distillery, its operation and most of all, the people who have all contributed to making it the success that it undoubtedly is today.

I have produced a lengthy list of all bottlings issued from the distillery, correct at the time of publishing, but have not included the multitude of single casks which the distillery has produced over the years. I am indebted to Hans-Peter and Berit Neumann who produce the Kilchomania website (www.kilchomania.com), which contains a full list of all these bottles and the single casks, updated daily and is a great source of information for all things happening at Kilchoman.

Kilchoman Distillery Bottlings

Release	Cask-No.	Distilled	Bottled	Strength	Age	Cask Type
General and Limited Releases						
Inaugural Release		2006	2009	46.0%	3 yo	Bourbon Barrels and Oloroso Sherry Casks

Autumn 2009 Release		2006	2009	46.0%	3 yo	Bourbon Barrels and Oloroso Sherry Casks
Spring 2010 Release		2006	2010	46.0%	3 yo	Bourbon Barrels and Oloroso Sherry Casks
Summer 2010 Release			2010	46.0%	3 yo	Fresh and Refill Bourbon Barrels
Winter 2010 Release		2007	2010	46.0%	3 yo	Fresh and Refill Bourbon Barrels
Spring 2011 Release		2007	March 2011	46.0%	3 yo	Fresh and Refill Bourbon Barrels
100% Islay, Inaugural Release		2008	2011	50.0%	3 yo	Fresh and Refill Bourbon Barrels
100% Islay, Inaugural Release Cask Strength	100-103/ 2008	2008	2011	61.3%	3 yo	Fresh and Refill Bourbon Barrels
100% Islay, 2nd Edition		2008, 2009	2012	50.0%	3 yo	Fresh and Refill Bourbon Barrels
100% Islay, 3rd Edition			2013	50.0%	4 yo	Fresh Bourbon Barrels
100% Islay, 4th Edition			2014	50.0%	4 yo	Fresh Bourbon Barrels
100% Islay, 5th Edition		2009, 2010	2015	50.0%	5 yo	Fresh and Refill Bourbon Barrels
100% Islay, 6th Edition		2010	2016	50.0%	6 yo	Fresh and Refill Bourbon Barrels
100% Islay, 7th Edition		2010	2017	50.0%	7 yo	Fresh and Refill Bourbon Barrels
100% Islay, 8th Edition		2008-2012	2018	50.0%		Bourbon Barrels, Oloroso Sherry Butts
100% Islay, 9th Edition		2008-2010	2019	50.0%	9 yo	Fresh and Refill Bourbon Barrels

100% Islay, 10th Edition		2008-2011	2020	50.0%	9 yo	Bourbon Barrels, Oloroso Sherry Butts
100% Islay, 11th Edition		2008-2012	2021	50.0%	9 yo	Bourbon Barrels, Oloroso Sherry Butts
100% Islay, 12th Edition		2012-2014	2022	50.0%	8 yo	Bourbon Barrels, Oloroso Sherry Butts
100% Islay, 13th Edition		2013-2015	2023	50.0%	8 yo	Bourbon Barrels
100% Islay, 14th Edition		2014-2015	2024	50.0%	9 yo	Bourbon Barrels, Oloroso Sherry Butts
(1st) Sherry Cask Release			2012	46.0%	4 yo	Oloroso Sherry Butts
Loch Gorm 2013		2007	2013	46.0%	5 yo	Oloroso Sherry Butts, Hogshead Finish
Loch Gorm 2014		2009	2014	46.0%	5 yo	Oloroso Sherry Butts
Loch Gorm 2015		2010	2015	46.0%	5 yo	Oloroso Sherry Butts and Hogsheads
Loch Gorm 2016		2010	2016	46.0%	6 yo	Oloroso Sherry Butts
Loch Gorm 2017		2009	2017	46.0%	7 yo	Oloroso Sherry Butts
Loch Gorm 2018		2007-2011	2018	46.0%	6 yo	Oloroso, Sherry Butts
Loch Gorm 2019		2006-2011	2019	46.0%	7 yo	Oloroso Sherry Butts
Loch Gorm 2020		2007-2011	2020	46.0%	8 yo	Oloroso Sherry Butts
Loch Gorm 2021		2011-2012	2021	46.0%	9 yo	Oloroso Sherry Butts
Loch Gorm 2022		2007-2013	2022	46.0%	8 yo	Oloroso Sherry Butts
Loch Gorm 2023		2013-2015	2023	46.0%	7 yo	Oloroso Sherry Butts
Loch Gorm 2024		2014	2024	46.0%	9 yo	Oloroso Sherry Butts

Machir Bay 2012			2012	46.0%	3 yo	Bourbon Barrels and Oloroso Sherry Casks
Machir Bay 2013			2013	46.0%	4 yo	Bourbon Barrels and Oloroso Sherry Casks
Machir Bay 2014			2014	46.0%	5 yo	Bourbon Barrels and Oloroso Sherry Casks
Machir Bay (General Release, since 2015)			2015	46.0%	NAS	Bourbon Barrels and Oloroso Sherry Casks
Machir Bay Cask Strength Limited Festive Edition			2020	58.6%	NAS	Bourbon Barrels and Oloroso Sherry Casks
Machir Bay Cask Strength Limited 2021 Edition			2022	58.3%	NAS	Bourbon Barrels and Oloroso Sherry Casks
Machir Bay Cask Strength European Tour 2014			2014	59.2%	NAS	Bourbon Barrels and Oloroso Sherry Casks
Machir Bay Cask Strength Land Rover UK Tour 2014			2014	58.8%	NAS	Bourbon Barrels and Oloroso Sherry Casks
Machir Bay Cask Strength 10th Anniversary Tour 2015			2015	58.9%	NAS	Bourbon Barrels and Oloroso Sherry Casks
Machir Bay Cask Strength Land Rover UK Tour 2015			2015	59.0%	NAS	Bourbon Barrels and Oloroso Sherry Casks
Machir Bay Cask Strength USA East Coast Tour 2016			2016	60.1%	NAS	Bourbon Barrels and Oloroso Sherry Casks
Machir Bay Cask Strength USA East Coast Tour 2017			2017	60.0%	NAS	Bourbon Barrels and Oloroso Sherry Casks

Machir Bay Cask Strength European Tour 2018			2018	59.8%	NAS	Bourbon Barrels and Oloroso Sherry Casks
Machir Bay Cask Strength Meet the Peat Tour 2019			2019	58.6%	NAS	Bourbon Barrels and Oloroso Sherry Casks
2023 European Tour Bottling			2023	58.5%	NAS	80% Bourbon 20% Port Casks
Pedro Ximénez Small Batch Bottled in collaboration with Land Rover			2023	51.3%	NAS	40% Bourbon 60% PX Casks
Coull Point			2013	46.0%	4 yo	Bourbon Barrels and Oloroso Sherry Casks
Saligo Bay			2014	46.0%	5 yo	Bourbon Barrels
Sanaig (2015)			2015	46.0%	NAS	Bourbon Barrels and Oloroso Sherry Casks
Sanaig (General Release, since 2016)			2016-	46.0%	NAS	Bourbon Barrels and Oloroso Sherry Casks
Sanaig Cask Strength 2024 Edition			10-2024	57.8%	NAS	Oloroso Sherry Casks & Bourbon Barrels with Oloroso Finish
Loch Gruinart			2020	46.0%	NAS	Bourbon Barrels, Oloroso and PX Sherry Casks
Loch Gruinart M&S Collection			2023	46.0%	NAS	Bourbon Barrels, Oloroso & PX Sherry Casks
Vintage 2006		2006	2011	46.0%	5 yo	Fresh and Refill Bourbon Barrels

Vintage 2007		2007	2013	46.0%	6 yo	Fresh and Refill Bourbon Barrels
Vintage 2008		2008	2015	46.0%	7 yo	Fresh and Refill Bourbon Barrels
Vintage 2009		2008/ 2009	2017	46.0%	8 yo	Fresh and Refill Bourbon Barrels, Oloroso Sherry Butts
Vintage 2010		2010	2019	48.0%	9 yo	Fresh and Refill Bourbon Barrels, Oloroso Sherry Butts
Original Cask Strength Release		2009	2014	59.2%	5 yo	Bourbon Barrels
Original Cask Strength – Quarter Cask		2010	2016	56.9%	6 yo	Quarter Casks
Port Cask Release		2011	2014	55.0%	3 yo	Ruby Port Casks
Port Cask Matured, 2018 Edition		2014	2018	50.0%	3 yo	Ruby Port Casks
Madeira Cask Release		2011	2015	50.0%	4 yo	Madeira Casks
10th Anniversary Release		2005-2012	2015	58.2%	3 yo	Bourbon Barrels & Oloroso Sherry Casks
Sauternes Cask Release		11/2010- 01/2011	2016	50.0%	5 yo	Sauternes Casks
Sauternes Cask Finish 2018 Edition		2012	25.09.2018	50.0%	5 yo	Bourbon Barrels, Sauternes Cask Finish
Red Wine Release		2012	03.10.2017	50.0%	5 yo	Red Wine Casks
STR Cask Matured 2019 Edition		2012	23.04.2019	50.0%	7 yo	STR Casks
Am Bùrach		2009-2011	15.05.2020	46.0%	9 yo	Bourbon Barrels, Oloroso Sherry Casks, Port Casks
Fino Sherry Matured		2014, 2016	01.10.2020	46.0%	4 yo	Fino Sherry Butts

131

PX Sherry Cask Matured Edition		2013, 2015	2021	47.3%	5 yo	PX Hogsheads & Bourbon Barrels, PX Finish
Madeira Cask Matured 2021 Edition		2016	2021	50.0%	5 yo	Fresh Madeira Hogsheads
Casado Limited Release		2014	10/2022	46.0%	6 yo	Fresh Bourbon Barrels, married in Portuguese Red Wine vats
Cognac Cask Matured Limited 2023 Edition		2016	03/2023	50.0%	6 yo	Cognac Casks
Fino Sherry Limited 2023 Edition		2018	03/2023	50.0%	5 yo	Fino Sherry Butts
PX Sherry Limited 2023 Edition		2018	08/2023	50.0%	5 yo	PX Sherry Hogsheads
16 yo Limited Edition		2006, 2007	2023	50.0%	16 yo	Bourbon Barrels, Oloroso Sherry Casks
Batch Strength Release			2024	57.0%	NAS	Bourbon / Oloroso Sherry / Re-charred Wine casks
Batch Strength Release – European Tour Exclusive			2024	57.0%	NAS	Bourbon / Oloroso Sherry / Re-charred Wine casks
Sauternes Cask Matured 2024 Edition		2017, 2018	2024	50.0%	5 yo	1st Fill & 2nd Fill Sauternes Casks
Port Cask Matured			Autumn 2024	50.0%		Port wine casks
Fèis Ìle						
Fèis Ìle 2010 Release	113/2007	2007	2010	62.2%	3 yo	Fresh Bourbon Barrel
Fèis Ìle 2011 Release	31, 32/2006	2006	2011	59.5%	5 yo	Fresh Bourbon Barrels, Refill Oloroso Sherry Finish
Fèis Ìle 2012 Release	100-103/2008	2008	2012	58.5%	4 yo	Fresh Bourbon Barrels, Oloroso Sherry Finish

Fèis Île 2013 Release	246, 247/2008	2008	2013	60.1%	5 yo	Fresh Bourbon Barrels
Fèis Île 2014 Release	328 & 329/2009	2009	2014	58.7%	4 yo	Fresh Bourbon Barrels, Fino Sherry Finish
Fèis Île 2015 Release	245, 449 & 450/2008	2008	2015	58.2%	6 yo	Fresh Bourbon Barrels
Fèis Île 2016 Release	429/2007	2007	2016	56.6%	8 yo	Oloroso Sherry Butt
Fèis Île 2017 Release	324/2008 + 433/2009	2008, 2009	2017	58.0%	7 yo	Bourbon Barrel & Oloroso Sherry Butt
Fèis Île 2018 Release	34, 65, 82, 83/2007	2007	2018	55.5%	11 yo	Bourbon Barrels
Fèis Île 2019 Release	141/2007, 80/2008	2007, 2008	2019	54.4%	11 yo	Fresh Bourbon Barrel & Fresh Oloroso Sherry Butt
Fèis Île 2020 Release	257/07, 260/07, 353/07, 359/07, 365/07, 141/08, 143/08, 163/08, 166/08, 168/08, 171/08	2007, 2008	2020	54.2%	12 yo	Bourbon Barrels
Fèis Île 2021 Release	94/2011, 151/2011; 27/2012, 711-714/2012, 718/2012	2011, 2012	2021	56.3%	8 yo	Bourbon Barrels & Oloroso Sherry Butts
Fèis Île 2022 Release	01/2006, 04/2006, 08/2006, 21/2006, 27/2006	2006	2022	52.1%	16 yo	Fresh Bourbon Barrels
Fèis Île 2023 Release		2012, 2013	2023	55.3%	10 yo	Fresh Bourbon Barrels, Oloroso Sherry Butt
Fèis Île 2024 Release	303/2011, 305/2011	08.06.2011	23.05.2024	53.0%	12 yo	Fresh Bourbon Barrels

133

Kilchoman Club						
Kilchoman Club, 1st Edition	451/2007	2007	2012	59.2%	5 yo	Oloroso Sherry Butt
Kilchoman Club, 2nd Edition	485-490, 567, 568/2008	2008	2013	58.2%	5 yo	Fresh Bourbon Barrels, Oloroso Sherry Finish
Kilchoman Club, 3rd Edition	65 & 66/2010	2010	2014	58.4%	4 yo	Fresh Madeira Casks
Kilchoman Club, 4th Edition	740 & 790/2010 & 28/2011	2010 & 2011	2015	60.0%	4 yo	Sauternes Wine Casks
Kilchoman Club, 5th Edition	227 & 308/2006	2006	2016	57.0%	10 yo	Fresh Bourbon Barrel & Fresh Oloroso Sherry Butt
Kilchoman Club, 6th Edition	383-385, 387, 388/2007	2007	2017	57.4%	10 yo	Fresh Bourbon Barrels
Kilchoman Club, 7th Edition	309 & 310/2006	2006	2018	55.2%	12 yo	Oloroso Sherry Butts
Kilchoman Club, 8th Edition	283/2006, 376, 123 & 425/2007	2006 & 2007	2019	54.3%	11 yo	Fresh Bourbon Barrels & Oloroso Sherry Butt
Kilchoman Club, 9th Edition	548-551/2012	2012	2020	56.2%	8 yo	Oloroso Sherry Hogsheads
Kilchoman Club, 10th Edition	634, 636, 640/2008	2008	2021	52.6%	12 yo	Oloroso Sherry Casks
Kilchoman Club, 11th Edition	45 & 47/2013, 1014/2014	2013 & 2014	2022	53.0%	7 yo	Bourbon Barrels, Marsala Cask Finish
Kilchoman Club, 12th Edition	1101/2016 & 1110/2016	26.11.2016 30.11.2016	30.11.2023	54.1%	7 yo	Bourbon Barrels, Blanc de Blancs Cask Finish
Kilchoman Club, 13th Edition	209/2015	01.04.2015	01.11.2024	57.2%	9 yo	Fresh Oloroso Sherry Butt

Comraich						
Comraich Batch No. 1	146/2007, 265/2007, 419/2007	2007	2017	55.5%	9 yo	Bourbon Barrels, Oloroso Sherry Butt
Comraich Batch No. 2	206, 207, 208/2011	2011	2019	55.3%	7 yo	Fresh Bourbon Barrels
Comraich Batch No. 3	524/2008, 528/2008, 275/2010	2008 & 2010	2019	55.7%	9 yo	Fresh Bourbon Barrels, Oloroso Sherry Butt
Comraich Batch No. 4	205/2011, 467/2011, 775/2011	2011	2021	55.0%	9 yo	Bourbon Barrels
Comraich Batch No. 5	460, 479, 480, 484/2014	2014	2022	55.5%	7 yo	Port Hogsheads
Comraich Batch No. 6	177/2011, 179/2011, 505/2012, 506/2012	2011 & 2012	2022	53.8%	10 yo	Bourbon Barrels, Calvados Cask Finish
Comraich Batch No. 7			16.08.2024	48.0%	8 yo	Bourbon barrels
Small Batch Releases for Selected Markets						
Belgium Small Batch No. 1			17.09.2019	48,9%	NAS	70% Bourbon, 5% Oloroso Sherry, 25% STR
Belgium Small Batch No. 2			17.03.2021	48,4%	NAS	70% Bourbon, 5% Oloroso Sherry, 25% PX
Belgium & Luxembourg Small Batch No. 3			19.10.2022	49,6%	NAS	70% [recte: 75%] Bourbon, 5% Oloroso Sherry, 20% Sauternes
China Small Batch No. 1			06.08.2019	48,2%	NAS	70% Bourbon, 5% Oloroso Sherry, 25% Port
China Small Batch No. 2			04.04.2021	49,0%	NAS	70% Bourbon / 10% Oloroso Sherry / 20% Sauternes

135

China Small Batch No. 3			2022	49,5%	NAS	70% Bourbon, 5% Oloroso Sherry, 25% Calvados
China Small Batch No. 4			2023	48.2%	NAS	75% Bourbon, 5% Oloroso Sherry, 20% STR
Finland Small Batch No. 1			06.06.2019	46.0%	NAS	80% Bourbon, 20% Oloroso Sherry
Finland Small Batch No. 2			13.05.2020	49.4%	NAS	70% Bourbon, 5% Oloroso Sherry, 25% Port
Finland Small Batch No. 3			16.03.2021	47.5%	NAS	70% Bourbon, 5% Oloroso Sherry, 25% Madeira
Bourbon Barrel Small Batch (for Finland) Turve	950/2015, 951/2015	2015	08.04.2022	56.0%	NAS	Fresh Bourbon Barrels
Exclusive Selection No. 1 (Small Batch Release for Le Comptoir Irlandais, France)			04.09.2019	46.8%	NAS	85% Bourbon, 15% Oloroso Sherry
Exclusive Selection No. 2 (Small Batch Release for Le Comptoir Irlandais, France)			04.09.2020	47.1%	NAS	80% Bourbon, 20% Oloroso Sherry
Exclusive Selection No. 2 [2021] (Small Batch Release for Le Comptoir Irlandais, France)			09.06.2021	47.2%	NAS	25% Sauternes % 70% Bourbon / 5% Oloroso Sherry
Le Comptoir Irlandais Small Batch – Cognac			20.09.2022	50.6%	NAS	70% Bourbon / 5% Oloroso Sherry / 25% Cognac

136

Le comptoir Irlandais Small Batch – Fino			21.09.2022	49.2%	NAS	70% Bourbon / 5% Oloroso Sherry / 25% Fino Sherry
French Inspiration #1 (Small Batch Release for France)			06.04.2022	49.7%	NAS	70% Bourbon / 5% Oloroso Sherry / 25% Calvados
French Inspiration #2 (Small Batch Release for France)			07.04.2022	49.1%	NAS	75% Bourbon / 5% Oloroso Sherry / 20% Sauternes
Triskele Casks French Exclusive No. 1			06.04.2023	48.6%	NAS	75% Bourbon / 5% Oloroso Sherry / 20% STR
Triskele Casks French Exclusive No. 2			07.04.2023	47,6%	NAS	75% Bourbon / 5% Oloroso Sherry / 20% Port
Germany Small Batch No. 1			13.06.2019	48.9%	NAS	70% Bourbon, 5% Oloroso Sherry, 25% Port
Genesis – Harvest, Stage 1			24.09.2020	48.6%	NAS	70% Bourbon, 10% Oloroso Sherry, 20% PX
Genesis – Malting, Stage 2			22.11.2021	49.2%	NAS	75% Bourbon, 5% Oloroso Sherry, 20% Sauternes
Genesis – Peating, Stage 3			16.11.2022	49.4%	NAS	70% Bourbon, 5% Oloroso Sherry, 25% STR Cask
Genesis – Mashing Stage 4			21.09.2023	49.1%	NAS	75% Bourbon, 5% Oloroso Sherry, 20% Cognac Cask
Triple Cask Matured Small Batch for Whisky.de			06.2022	46.0%	NAS	75% Bourbon, 5% Oloroso, 20% PX
Triskele Casks – Italian Exclusive 2023/1			24.10.2023	48.3%	NAS	75% Bourbon, 5% Oloroso Sherry, 20% STR

Japan Small Batch No. 1			03.02.2020	48.1%	NAS	70% Bourbon, 5% Oloroso Sherry, 25% Madeira
Japan Small Batch No. 2			2022	50.1%	NAS	70% Bourbon, 5% Oloroso Sherry, 25% Calvados
Korea Small Batch No. 1			07.04.2022	49.0%	NAS	75% Bourbon / 5% Oloroso Sherry / 20% Sauternes
The Netherlands Small Batch No. 1			27.06.2019	47.0%	NAS	85% Bourbon, 5% Oloroso Sherry, 10% PX
The Netherlands Small Batch No. 2			08.07.2020	49.4%	NAS	70% Bourbon, 5% Oloroso Sherry, 25% Madeira
Netherlands Small Batch No. 3			16.06.2022	49.3%	NAS	70% Bourbon, 5% Oloroso Sherry, 25% STR
Triskele Casks Netherlands Exclusive 2023-1			03.10.2023	48.7%	NAS	Bourbon, Oloroso Sherry, Sauternes
Norway Small Batch No. 1			2021	48.8%	NAS	75% Bourbon, 5% Oloroso Sherry, 20% PX
Norway Small Batch No. 2			2022	48.9%	NAS	75% Bourbon, 5% Oloroso Sherry, 20% Sauternes
Poland Small Batch No. 1			30.06.2021	47.6%	NAS	70% Bourbon, 5% Oloroso Sherry, 25% Sauternes
Poland Small Batch No. 2			20.09.2022	49.3%	NAS	75% Bourbon, 5% Oloroso Sherry, 20% Sauternes
Quebec Small Batch No. 1			31.08.2022	49.1%	NAS	75% Bourbon, 5% Oloroso Sherry, 20% Sauternes

Triskele Casks Exclusivité Quèbec			29.11.2023	48.9%	NAS	70% Bourbon, 5% Oloroso Sherry, 25% Calvados
Small Batch Release STR / Bourbon / Sherry [for Smaller Markets]			20.03.2023	48.7%	NAS	75% Bourbon, 5% Oloroso Sherry, 20% STR
Sweden Small Batch No. 1			12.09.2019	47.2%	NAS	85% Bourbon, 15% Oloroso Sherry
Sweden Small Batch No. 2			28.10.2021	48,4%	NAS	75% Bourbon, 5% Oloroso Sherry, 20% Sauternes
Sweden Small Batch No. 3			21.09.2022	48.2%	NAS	75% Bourbon, 5% Oloroso Sherry, 20% PX Sherry
Triskele Casks – Sweden Exclusive			06.09.2023	48.2%	NAS	75% Bourbon, 5% Oloroso Sherry, 20% STR
Taiwan Small Batch No. 1			11.2019	46.9%	NAS	85% Bourbon, 5% Oloroso Sherry, 10% PX Sherry
Taiwan Small Batch No. 2				48.7%	NAS	75% Bourbon, 5% Oloroso Sherry, 20% PX Sherry
Taiwan Small Batch No. 3			2023	48.8%	NAS	75% Bourbon, 5% Oloroso Sherry, 25% Calvados
UK Small Batch No. 1			29.10.2019	48.3%	NAS	70% Bourbon, 5% Oloroso Sherry, 25% Madeira
UK Small Batch No. 2			06.08.2020	47.4%	NAS	70% Bourbon, 20% PX, 10% Oloroso Sherry
UK Small Batch No. 3			16.11.2021	49.1%	NAS	70% Bourbon, 5% Oloroso Sherry, 25% Sauternes

139

UK Small Batch No. 4			19.07.2022	49.8%	NAS	70% Bourbon, 5% Oloroso Sherry, 25% STR
UK Small Batch No. 5			31.03.2023	49.0%	NAS	70% Bourbon, 5% Oloroso Sherry, 25% Calvados
USA Small Batch No. 1			15.08.2019	48.5%	NAS	70% Bourbon, 5% Oloroso Sherry, 25% Port
USA Small Batch No. 2			18.02.2020	48.5%	NAS	70% Bourbon, 5% Oloroso Sherry, 25% Madeira
USA Small Batch No. 3			20.08.2020	48.9%	NAS	50% Port, 47% Bourbon, 3% Oloroso Sherry
USA Small Batch No. 4			03.12.2020	48.1%	NAS	65% Bourbon, 5% Oloroso Sherry, 30% Madeira
USA Small Batch No. 5			07.05.2021	48.3%	NAS	70% Bourbon, 5% Oloroso Sherry, 25% Sauternes
USA Small Batch No. 6			2021	47.9%	NAS	70% Bourbon, 5% Oloroso, 25% PX
USA Small Batch No. 7			2022	50.0%	NAS	70% Bourbon, 5% Oloroso, 25% STR
USA Small Batch No. 8			2023	47.7%	NAS	75% Bourbon / 5% Oloroso Sherry / 20% Port
B.I.B. Bourbon Influenced Batch [for the USA]			06.05.2021	50.0%	9 yo	Wheated Bourbon Barrels
Spec´s Small Batch No. 1			06.2022	50.3%	NAS	70% Bourbon, 5% Oloroso Sherry, 25% Calvados
Total Wine Concierge Small Batch No. 2			06.2022	49.7%	NAS	70% Bourbon, 5% Oloroso Sherry, 25% Sauternes

Triskele Casks [Small Batch] for Spec's – Sauternes			2023	49,2%	NAS	75% Bourbon, 5% Oloroso Sherry, 20% Sauternes
Triskele Casks [Small Batch] for Spec's – STR			2023	49,3%	NAS	75% Bourbon, 5% Oloroso Sherry, 20% STR
Other Small Batch Releases						
Small Batch Release, Sherry Finish		10.2008	30.11.2013	58.2%	5 yo	Fresh Bourbon Barrels, Oloroso Sherry Finish
Small Batch Release, Fresh Bourbon		03 & 08.2011	03.2017	58.3%	5 yo	Fresh Bourbon Barrels
Small Batch Release, Fresh Bourbon		06.2011	18.07.2017	55.7%	6 yo	Fresh Bourbon Barrels
Small Batch Release, Bourbon and PX Sherry Finish	76, 214, 622, 627/2012	2012	23.04.2018	57.8%	5 yo	Fresh Bourbon Barrels & PX Finish
Small Batch for Germany, Bourbon Cask	247-249/2007	15.08.2007	10.10.2012	59.3%	5 yo	Fresh Bourbon Barrels
Small Batch for Germany, Sherry Finish	392-394/2008	07.08.2008	07.10.2013	59.4%	5 yo	Fresh Bourbon Barrels, Oloroso Sherry Finish
Small Batch for Germany, 100% Islay	358-360/2009	30.07.2009	27.08.2014	60.7%	5 yo	Fresh Bourbon Barrels
Small Batch for Germany, PX Finish/Oloroso Casks	696,697/2010; 520/2011	01.09.2011	21.09.2016	58.2%	4 yo	Bourbon Barrels, PX Finish & Oloroso Sherry Cask
Small Batch for Germany, Oloroso Casks	185&186/ 2008	24.04.2008	22.02.2017	56.6%	8 yo	Oloroso Sherry Casks
Small Batch Rum Finish – Local Dealer Edition for Germany	143&142/ 2011, 403& 410/ 2012	17.03.2011 & 05.07.2012	03.10.2018	56.2%	6 yo	Bourbon Barrels, Jamaica Rum Finish

Small Batch PX Cask Finish Vatting for The Swedish Whisky Federation		2011 & 2012	20.09.2017	56.7%		Bourbon Barrels, PX Finish
[Small Batch] Commemorating the opening of the new still house & visitor centre 21st February 2020			13.02.2020	54.3%	11 yo	Fresh Bourbon Barrels, Oloroso Sherry Casks
10 yo Distillery Exclusive Small Batch Release 100% Islay			08.05.2024	50.0%	10 yo	60% Bourbon Barrels, 40% Oloroso Sherry Casks

www.ingramcontent.com/pod-product-compliance
Ingram Content Group UK Ltd.
Pitfield, Milton Keynes, MK11 3LW, UK
UKHW020017150725
460779UK00001B/1

9 781835 385913